ALL ABOUT SIX SIGMA

ALL ABOUT SIX SIGMA

The Easy Way to Get Started

WARREN BRUSSEE

McGraw-Hill

New York   Chicago   San Francisco   Lisbon   London
Madrid   Mexico City   Milan   New Delhi   San Juan
Seoul   Singapore   Sydney   Toronto

1 2 3 4 5 6 7 8 9 0   FGR/FGR   0 9 8 7 6 5

ISBN 0-07-145372-5

McGraw-Hill books are available at special discounts to use as premiums and sales promotions, or for use in corporate training programs. For more information, please write to the Director of Special Sales, Professional Publishing, McGraw-Hill, Two Penn Plaza, New York, NY 10121-2298. Or contact your local bookstore.

This publication is designed to provide accurate and authoritative information in regard to the subject matter covered. It is sold with the understanding that neither the author nor the publisher is engaged in rendering legal, accounting, futures/ securities trading, or other professional service. If legal advice or other expert assistance is required, the services of a competent professional person should be sought.
—*From a Declaration of Principles jointly adopted by a Committee of the American Bar Association and a Committee of Publishers*

This book is printed on recycled, acid-free paper containing a minimum of 50% recycled, de-inked paper.

Library of Congress Cataloging-in-Publication Data

Brussee, Warren.
    All about six sigma / Warren Brussee.
      p. cm.
    Includes bibliographical references and index.
    ISBN 0-07-145372-5 (alk. paper)
    1. Six sigma (Quality control standard)   2. Total quality management.   I. Title.
TS156.B775   2005
658.4'013—dc22   2005015797

To my wife Lois and my two children. They have never faltered in believing in me as I approached different challenges in life, including becoming an author. Belief in someone is a wonderful gift.

CONTENTS

PART SIX: CONTROLLING A PROCESS AND TEACHING SIX SIGMA

PART SEVEN: MISCELLANEOUS OTHER SIX SIGMA TOOLS—OVERVIEW

When I was getting my GE training in Six Sigma, there was an outside consultant teaching one of the Six Sigma tools, and it seemed that he was making it more complicated than required. After a few days of training, I asked him if some simplifications wouldn't be valid, with no loss of tool utility. He laughed, said he agreed, and even offered some thoughts on how the subject could be simplified even further than what I had suggested. I was taken aback with this answer and asked why, since he felt that way, he wasn't teaching a more simplified approach. His answer was that because he had his Ph.D. in mathematics, was an author of a book on the subject, and was being paid a lot of money by GE, he felt that the depth and complexity he was presenting was expected.

Since most of the existing books on Six Sigma were written by people similar to the instructor mentioned above, with very specialized and esoteric knowledge in their own academic fields, much of Six Sigma is presented in a more complex format than is really required.

Six Sigma enables companies to reduce costly defects. It uses data and logic to drive process improvements and to measure success. Although most Six Sigma work has been in manufacturing, Six Sigma is generic and has shown success in virtually any area that has quality issues.

This book demystifies Six Sigma. Although Six Sigma is being used in many companies, it is generally thought of as being complex and bureaucratic, requiring confusing software and statistics. This image is exacerbated by the acronyms and confusing terms used to describe the Six Sigma process. Even its title is misleading: "Six Sigma" is often defined as having a goal of 3 defects per million. As you will discover later, 3 defects per million is 4.5 sigma, *not* six sigma.

Six Sigma is similar to earlier quality programs such as Total Quality Control (TQC) and ISO 9000. The biggest differences are that Six Sigma is packaged better, is tied closely to bottom-line profits, and has gotten a high degree of support from top levels of management. In fact, GE's autocratic CEO Jack Welch's insistence on its use at GE did more to get Six Sigma recognized than any other contributing factor.

One misconception about Six Sigma is that every element of Six Sigma is complicated, requiring highly trained experts to implement. Not true! Many of the Six Sigma "tools" are straightforward and require no statistics. These tools are grounded in common sense and are structured to assist implementation. In fact, in this text the first 14 chapters require no probability or statistics.

Even when statistical work is needed to validate process differences or product changes, the statistical tools require no more math than what most people get in high school. However, this type of math is not used much in daily life, so some review and simplification are needed. Chapters requiring statistics have practical practice problems with detailed steps. The 10 formulas and 4 tables included in this book are all someone need to be able to do the statistics required for the Six Sigma work described here. Microsoft's *Excel* has all the needed software.

Many of the Six Sigma tools in this text are labeled as "simplified." This simplification does not reduce their effectiveness; it just puts a degree of reality into the tools. In all cases I give reasons for the simplifications and give reference texts for those wishing to use the traditional nonsimplified tools.

Most books on Six Sigma are just an overview, with little detail on actually *using* Six Sigma. *All About Six Sigma*, in contrast, takes the reader through the Six Sigma tool details and required statistics so that he or she can quickly apply Six Sigma to real-world problems.

This book assumes that the readers have little starting knowledge of Six Sigma. Perhaps their company is just beginning to implement this methodology and they want to get a head start. The goal of the book is that these people will be able to initiate and complete Six Sigma projects with the knowledge they glean from this book.

Of course, there are levels of Six Sigma that are beyond the scope of this book. Six Sigma black belts have skills in task-specific software and additional sophisticated tools. However, even black belts often use only the basic tools described in this book. Most real-world problems don't require complex problem-solving software or statistics.

Warren Brussee

ACKNOWLEDGMENTS

Many thanks to Bonnie Burnick, a Six Sigma black belt, and to Christopher Welker and Cheri Sims. This is the second Six Sigma book they have helped debug and improve. Also, thanks to all the people who gave me feedback on my earlier book on Six Sigma. Many of your inputs were taken into account in the writing of *All About Six Sigma*.

Two additional people were critical to this book, both with McGraw-Hill: Jeanne Glasser, senior editor, first suggested this book and kept me focused on the goal. Jane Palmieri, editing manager, miraculously turned my manuscript into this finished book. My sincere thanks to both.

Of course, any errors or omissions are mine, since I made the final determination in content.

ALL ABOUT
SIX SIGMA

Overview

Ab ovo   (From the very beginning)

—Latin saying

Part One, which includes Chapters 1 through 5, gives an overview of the whole Six Sigma methodology. This includes a brief history, starting with Motorola, and continuing on to its implementation at GE and at smaller companies. Management's role and the advantages and disadvantages of a strongly dictated company implementation are discussed.

Six Sigma involves teams. The makeup of these teams is critical, as is the acknowledgment of their contributions. Agreed-upon metrics, or measurements, are required to determine the severity of a problem and the progress of Six Sigma projects.

The Define, Measure, Analyze, Improve, and Control (DMAIC) problem-solving steps used for Six Sigma projects are reviewed in detail.

The History and Methodology of Six Sigma

What you will learn in this chapter is a brief history of Six Sigma, including the major companies that popularized it and the savings attributed to its use. We will also define the goal of the Six Sigma methodology with its emphasis on economically driven quality.

SIX SIGMA HISTORY

By one measure, Six Sigma started in 1809 when Carl Gauss published *Theoria Motus Corporum Arithmeticae*. In this book he introduced the concept of the *normal curve* (or the *Gaussian curve*) as being representative of the data from many processes. Since little of Six Sigma is new, it can be argued that Six Sigma is the cumulative result of all the quality initiatives that have been developed since Gauss's original concept. This would include the Simplified Process Control (SPC) and Total Quality Management (TQM) programs.

Motorola was the first large company to implement Six Sigma in the 1980s, and they developed much of the initial definition. Motorola decided that the traditionally used defects-per-thousand-parts quality measurement was not sufficiently sensitive and that the measurement needed to be defects per million parts. In this way people would not get a false sense that they were doing well because of a low defect-per-thousand quality score. The company also came up with a standard roadmap to use for Six Sigma problem solving, and they stressed that quality projects had to show a positive effect on the bottom line.

Other large companies, like Allied Signal, soon followed Motorola's lead, often putting their own spin on details of Six Sigma implementation. Since few books had been published on the subject, these companies developed their own in-house Six Sigma training manuals, with their own philosophies.

Jack Welch, CEO of GE, was in the hospital when he was visited by Larry Bossidy, CEO of Allied Signal. During his visit, Bossidy waxed poetic about the virtues of Six Sigma, and he told Welch of the savings Allied Signal had realized using this methodology. Apparently Welch got a vision, because when he got out of the hospital, he began implementing Six Sigma at GE with a vengeance. The result was that GE was the company that finally pushed Six Sigma "over the top," making Six Sigma a recognized process.

The attraction to Six Sigma comes from its bottom-line emphasis. Six Sigma–generated savings of $16 billion have been claimed at Motorola, $800 million at Allied Signal, and $12 billion at GE in its first five years of use.

As Six Sigma was being integrated into these companies, many consultants started teaching Six Sigma. These consultants put their own interpretation into the methodology, so there has been an evolving definition of the *Six Sigma* process. There is no single standard of what is included in the Six Sigma methodology, nor is there an agreement of what Six Sigma tools apply. However, the Six Sigma tools included in this text represent the consensus of most current Six Sigma practitioners.

Today there are more than a hundred books on Six Sigma and the Six Sigma tools. Many of these books have supporting software, so there is no lack of reference material. Many technical schools across the country offer classes in Six Sigma, and these classes are often taught by former GE or Allied Signal Six Sigma black belts. The American Society of Quality offers classes and certifications in Six Sigma, so the awareness and acceptance of Six Sigma have become widespread.

Because of its perceived level of complexity and required computer software, the use of Six Sigma has been mainly concentrated in large companies. However, what you will learn in this text is that its application possibilities are far broader. Medium- and small-sized companies are now beginning to incorporate Six Sigma, and it is also being used in nonindustrial settings.

THE GOAL OF THE SIX SIGMA METHODOLOGY

What differentiates Six Sigma from other quality initiatives is that it emphasizes that quality programs have to be economically viable. An improvement in quality that doesn't drive profits does not fit into the Six Sigma philosophy. However, because Six Sigma does improve profitability, funding and support for these programs are ensured.

DEFINITION

The goal of Six Sigma methodology   The Six Sigma methodology uses a *specific problem-solving approach* and *selected Six Sigma tools* to improve processes and products. This methodology is data driven, and the goal is to reduce unacceptable products or events.

The original goal of the Six Sigma methodology was to reduce process variation such that the number of unacceptable products would be no more than 3 defects per million parts. As currently practiced by most companies, however, the real-world application of Six Sigma is to make a product that satisfies the customer and minimizes supplier losses to the point at which it is *not cost effective to pursue tighter quality.*

If you were to buy a box of 500 paper clips and one of them was incorrectly bent, would you be upset? Probably not. Nor would you be likely to switch suppliers for your paper clips. Yet, if this defect rate were consistent for *all* the boxes of paper clips, the defect rate would be 2,000 defects per million parts, which is a far cry from 3 defects per million. It may very well be that 2,000 defects per million is an acceptable defect level for paper clips, and it may not be economically viable to try to improve that rate. The correct defect goal will vary based on the product and both the supplier's and customer's costs and needs.

Even though the defect goal may vary, the Six Sigma methodology still applies for getting the defect rate down to the most acceptable (and economical) level. Six Sigma works no matter what the targeted defect level; in fact, Six Sigma tools help define what that target should be.

CHAPTER 1 REVIEW

1. Motorola was the first large company to implement Six Sigma in the 1980s, and they developed much of the initial definition.

2. Other large companies, like Allied Signal and GE, soon followed Motorola's lead. Today many medium and small companies are beginning to implement Six Sigma.

3. Because of the perceived level of complexity and the computer software it requires, the use of Six Sigma has been concentrated mainly in large companies.

4. The Six Sigma tools included in this text represent the tools used today by most current Six Sigma practitioners.

5. The Six Sigma methodology uses a *specific problem-solving approach* and *select Six Sigma tools* to improve processes and products.

6. The name *Six Sigma* refers to the goal of reducing defects to 3 parts per million.

7. A more realistic goal is to make a product that satisfies the customer and minimizes supplier losses to the point at which it is not cost effective to pursue tighter quality. This is the current philosophy of Six Sigma.

Management's Role

What you will learn in this chapter is that it is easiest to implement Six Sigma when it has active management support, but it is also possible for an energetic individual to implement Six Sigma from the "bottom up." In fact, dictatorial introduction by management is *not* ideal because people are less likely to embrace the methodology for its real value. Also, the pressure to make Six Sigma succeed can cause projects to incorrectly be claimed as Six Sigma, which can stir up resentment against the methodology.

COMMITMENT OF TOP MANAGEMENT

It is easiest to implement Six Sigma in an organization in which the commitment is demonstrated through company-wide communications explaining the process and its goals, with some explanation on why the company is going to invest the time and manpower to implement the Six Sigma methodology. This level of buy-in demonstrates to the whole company that management believes in this methodology. The required investment in people and training is then likely to happen, along with everyone's active participation.

The company should also demonstrate its support of Six Sigma by taking into account an employee's use and expertise in Six Sigma when determining promotional potential. This is *not* the same as GE's insistence that someone *had* to be highly skilled in Six

Sigma to be even considered for promotion. At GE, when Six Sigma was first introduced, this Six Sigma expertise requirement caused some perceived unjustified promotions, bypassing people more qualified who had not yet achieved full Six Sigma expertise. This caused some negative reaction to Six Sigma.

When incorporating Six Sigma, many companies start out using outside consultants and/or instructors, then transition to in-house people as trainers. The only issue with this approach arises when the consultant uses a nonstandard text for instruction because then the in-house people must originate course material or work from the consultant's homegrown course material.

SIX SIGMA SEPARATE

Some companies set up Six Sigma as a separate organization, which then services the rest of the company. The separate organization works in parallel with existing groups, identifying and implementing Six Sigma projects in addition to any current projects. All Six Sigma projects are funneled through the separate Six Sigma organization.

The advantage of this approach is that Six Sigma success can be readily measured. The downside is that the separate Six Sigma organization is often looked upon as a group of prima donnas, with their own set of agendas. This causes some degree of resentment among others in the organization and stifles cooperation. It also discourages "expert" input into Six Sigma projects since many of these experts feel threatened. There can also be some feeling that current ideas are "stolen" and then labeled as "Six Sigma."

SIX SIGMA INTEGRATED

An alternate approach is to incorporate Six Sigma as part of the current company structure, without a separate Six Sigma organization. Six Sigma then becomes an integral part of everyone's job, using a relatively few highly trained Six Sigma people as reference instructors. This makes it somewhat more difficult to measure the effect of Six Sigma, but it inspires a common Six Sigma language and philosophy that will then permeate the organization. As the Six Sigma methodology unfolds in the coming chapters, it will be seen that Six Sigma is helpful to everyone in the organization and therefore it *should* become an integral part of everyone's job.

GE started with Six Sigma as a separate organization but then gradually transitioned to an integrated approach because of the issues noted above.

SIX SIGMA FROM THE BOTTOM UP

Sometimes a high-level manager, or the overall company management, feels that the company can't afford the training, software, computer upgrades, and so on, that they believe are required to implement Six Sigma. Management may also be dubious about whether the skill level in the company will support the perceived technical competence required. In these cases, complete management buy-in is unlikely. In this environment it may be necessary for dynamic individuals or teams to start this process from the bottom up.

Many Six Sigma tools will work independently, without company-wide incorporation. The tools can also be simplified, as shown in this text, and do not require the esoteric software often associated with Six Sigma. Many of the tools require no statistics; for those tools that do, *Excel* is sufficient for all calculations and graphs. Even the implementation of two or three Six Sigma tools can make a measurable difference in a company's performance.

Of course, any individuals planning to use Six Sigma on their own initiative should first review the plans with their manager; usually a manager will not discourage this extra effort. There may be a caveat from the manager that no additional costs should occur and no ongoing projects should be delayed.

After someone has demonstrated the success of Six Sigma, others will often follow the lead. Then expanded tool use and training can occur. Although this takes personal initiative on the part of the person introducing Six Sigma, it is a great way to get noticed and truly influence a company's success. Even when a company's management *is* supportive of Six Sigma, it generally takes a few dynamic individuals to lead.

Although this bottom-up approach is possible, full management support from the start is preferable and more likely to result in company-wide implementation of Six Sigma.

SIX SIGMA: QUALITY PROGRAM FLAVOR OF THE MONTH?

Whenever a new quality or production methodology is introduced into a company, many people tend to dismiss it as just another management *flavor of the month*. This is because they have seen many programs come and go, periodically replaced with whatever is the current fad. They have seen programs such as Total Quality Management (TQM), ISO 9000, Kepner-Trego, Workout, Ishikawa Diagrams, Zero Defects, Kaizen, and Quality Circles be introduced with much fanfare, with the assurance that the introduced program is *forever*! But *forever* seems to be rather short in duration.

These programs falter for many reasons, foremost among them being the lack of a long-term commitment by management caused by no realized and quick bottom-line profits.

Can Six Sigma fail for the same reasons? Of course! But Six Sigma has several things going for it that the other programs do not, with the biggest advantage being its emphasis on profits. As long as a company is seeing measurable financial benefits from the program, they will give it their continuing support.

Another way Six Sigma can fail is when it is made to be too complex. If people are overwhelmed with complex statistics and software, they will give the program only lip service. It will be abandoned as soon as management takes their eye off the Six Sigma ball. But if the training in Six Sigma is successful and the concept is simplified for people, everyone in the company will start using at least some of the tools as part of their normal approach to problems. The advantages of the Six Sigma tools will be so apparent that people will use them to make their jobs easier, and the rewards that come from successful projects will follow.

CHAPTER 2 REVIEW

1. It is easiest to implement Six Sigma in an organization in which there is complete commitment to it from top management, but autocratic support is not required.

2. Although complete corporate commitment is desirable, many Six Sigma tools can be used independently to make substantial improvements. This approach allows for

bottom-up acceptance of Six Sigma. *It is not necessary to implement all the tools to have a measurable effect on reducing defects.*

3. Some companies set up Six Sigma as a separate organization. This can cause some animosity. A preferred approach is to incorporate Six Sigma into the existing organization as an integral part of everyone's current job.

Six Sigma Titles and Teams

This chapter defines the Six Sigma titles of green belt, black belt, and master black belt. It also explains the importance of team makeup when implementing a Six Sigma project. The Six Sigma team should include representatives from every area potentially affected by the project, including customers.

SIX SIGMA TITLES

DEFINITIONS

Green belt A Six Sigma *green belt* is the primary implementer or team leader of the Six Sigma methodology. He or she earns this title by taking classes in Six Sigma, demonstrating competency on Six Sigma tests, and implementing Six Sigma projects.

Black belt A Six Sigma *black belt* has Six Sigma skills sufficient to enable him or her to act as an instructor, mentor, and expert reference to green belts. A black belt is also competent in additional Six Sigma tool-specific software programs and statistics.

Master black belt A Six Sigma *master black belt* generally has management responsibility for Six Sigma when it is set up as a separate organization.

A team leader will normally be a green belt. The training and experience required to become a green belt vary among companies. However, most companies require some classroom training along with completion of several recognized Six Sigma projects. There are also outside firms that train, test, and then "ordain" someone as a green belt or black belt. Other team members will normally be trained as needed by the green belt, with training applicable to each team member's involvement in the Six Sigma project.

TEAM COMPOSITION

Six Sigma projects are not accomplished by lone individuals but by teams of people working together. Some team members will be Six Sigma experts, some will be process experts, some will be data gatherers, and others will be users and customers. There could be production, maintenance, design, and management people involved. The team makeup will vary, based on the need and stage of each Six Sigma project. One constant throughout the Six Sigma project will be the team leader, who will usually be a green belt.

What should never be overlooked or bypassed in any Six Sigma project is the acknowledgment of each team member's contribution to the project. And the credit for the results obtained should be shared among all team members.

The most important feature of Six Sigma team composition is that all areas affected by the project be represented. The importance of making this list all-inclusive may seem obvious, but one of the qualities of creative people is that they often feel that they can "do it alone." Since these people have had some success with this loner approach, it is not always apparent to them that utilizing more inputs will make their successes even greater and that they will face fewer barriers in getting their ideas implemented. Many Six Sigma tools *require* the utilization of others' inputs.

Customers are sometimes ignored when setting up teams, and that is unfortunate because they often have unique insights into a project's needs and issues. The term *customer* doesn't apply to just the final user. Everyone that is affected by a process or product change is a customer. That could include the person producing, inspecting, or packing a product. It could include marketing and sales people, distributors, and, of course, the final users of a product. Consideration must be made as to which of these groups are affected by a proposed Six Sigma project or change, and team representation must include people from all these affected areas.

All Six Sigma team members should be involved in an initial meeting at which the project is outlined and everyone can see his or her own part in the total. At this meeting, the team leader gives a project overview, explains how he or she needs everyone's help, and promises that each member will get recognition for his or her efforts. There should be periodic updates with all team members. And, of course, there should be a final meeting where results are reviewed and everyone celebrates the project's success. The team leader should make sure that these meetings are well planned and as short as reasonably possible. People are busy and will resent it if their time is not effectively utilized.

Throughout the project there will be many mini-meetings with the appropriate team members involved in that particular project step. These mini-meetings do not replace the total team meetings.

If team members are treated with respect, kept updated on the project's progress, and given the proper recognition, they will look forward to being members of Six Sigma teams.

One caveat: Never have people be part of a Six Sigma team that has a goal of eliminating people in the team members' own specific work area. Not only will the project goal probably not be met but you will likely never get the members to be on another Six Sigma team.

CHAPTER 3 REVIEW

1. Six Sigma projects are not accomplished by individuals working in isolation but by many people working together in teams. The makeup of these teams of people will vary per project, based on need.

2. Companies that embrace the Six Sigma philosophy train people to various skill and responsibility levels and assign them the following titles: green belt, black belt, and master black belt. Green belts are often team leaders.

3. The training of the other team members will normally be done as needed by the green belt. The training will be applicable to each team member's involvement.

4. The most important feature of the team makeup is that all areas affected by the project are represented, including

customers. This not only ensures that the best and most knowledgeable input is obtained, but also that the project gets broad buy-in.

5. If team members are treated with respect, kept updated on the project's progress, and given the proper recognition, they will look forward to being on Six Sigma teams.

6. Never have people be part of a Six Sigma team that has a goal of eliminating people in the team members' own specific work area. Not only will the project goal probably not be met, but you will probably never get the members to be on another Six Sigma team.

CHAPTER 4

Metrics and Keeping Score

In this chapter you will learn that when doing a Six Sigma project, you have to establish a performance baseline at the start of the project. This enables you to see where you are, in terms of defects, and to know if you have made an improvement with your Six Sigma work.

Metrics, as the term is used by quality control types, means a system of measurement. There are many metrics used in industry, especially related to quality. In this text we will use three of the most common: defects per million (DPM), process sigma level, and defects per million opportunities (DPMO).

Defects per million parts (DPM) is the most common measurement of defect level, and it is the primary measurement used in this book. This metric closely relates to the bottom-line cost of defects because it labels a part as being simply good or bad, with no indication as to whether a part is bad due to multiple defects or due to a single defect. This metric also ignores where in the process the defect occurred. The part is just good or bad!

The *process sigma level* enables someone to project the DPM by analyzing a representative sample of a product. Also, it enables some comparison of relative defect levels between different processes. Process sigma level will be discussed in more detail later in the text.

Defects per million opportunities (DPMO) helps in identifying possible solutions because it identifies key problem areas rather than just labeling a part as bad.

For example, defining a defect *opportunity* on a part that is assembled on a production line requires identifying all the different defects that occur on the assembled part, how many places on that part the defects can occur, and every production step that the product goes through that could cause one or more of the defects.

Suppose a glass part has a crack or chip, both considered separate defects, occurring in any of 3 protrusions on the part. You identify 2 places in the process where the crack or chip could have occurred. This would be a total of 2 defects $\times$ 3 protrusions $\times$ 2 places = 12 opportunities for a protrusion crack or chip. Assume that at the end of the production line we see protrusion cracks or chips on 10 percent of the glass parts. The defects per opportunity would then be the 10 percent defect rate divided by the number of opportunities, or $0.1/12 = 0.008333$. If we want to convert this to DPMO, we must multiply the defects per opportunity by 1 million. This will give us a DPMO of 8,333.

The above example involves a manufactured product. However, DPMO applies to other areas. For example, on looking at *quantity errors* made on phone orders, a person ordering a quantity of an item could make a mistake when stating the number he or she wants, the person receiving the information could misunderstand the caller, the wrong quantity could be mistakenly entered into the order computer, or the person filling the order could misread the order or just send the wrong quantity. This is 5 different opportunities for the error. If quantities were entered on 2 separate items, there would be 10 opportunities for error. If errors occurred on 1 percent of orders involving 2 quantity inputs, the DPMO would be $0.01/10 \times 1,000,000$, which is a DPMO of 1,000.

If someone purchased a book and finds 25 misspelled words, assuming the book has 70,000 words, the defects per opportunity would be $25/70,000$, or 0.000357. Converting this to DPMO, it is $0.000357 \times 1,000,000$. This gives a DPMO of 357.

In the above misspelled-word example, we did not count individual letters within the word as being the opportunities. The customer was concerned with *misspelled words*, not *incorrect letters*.

The defect title usually gives direction as to how finitely you define the opportunity.

The purpose of the example above is to demonstrate that if you are using DPMO, you must carefully define exactly what defects you are including and exactly what you are calling a *defect opportunity*—otherwise you will be comparing apples to oranges.

CHAPTER 4 REVIEW

1. When doing a Six Sigma project, you have to establish a performance baseline. In this way you will be able to see where you are in terms of defects, and you will know if you make an improvement with your Six Sigma project.

2. *Metrics* means a system of measurements. In this text we use three metrics: defects per million (DPM), process sigma level, and defects per million opportunities (DPMO).

3. DPM most closely relates to the cost of defects because it labels a part as being simply good or bad and does not indicate whether a part is bad due to single or multiple defects. The DPM metric also ignores where in the process the defect has occurred. The part is just good or bad!

4. When using DPMO, you must be sure that the definitions of *defect* and *opportunity* are consistent throughout the study or project.

The DMAIC Problem-Solving Method

What you will learn in this chapter is the DMAIC problem-solving approach used by greenbelts. This is a generic plan that can be used on almost any type of problem. It gives discipline to the steps that someone should work through when attacking a problem, and it is the road map that is followed for all projects and process improvements. Which tools are used and what statistics are needed are dictated by each project. The appendix has a Six Sigma statistical tool finder matrix that can be used in determining which Six Sigma tool is most helpful for each DMAIC step.

DEFINITIONS

DMAIC problem-solving method: Define, Measure, Analyze, Improve, Control   This is the Six Sigma problem-solving approach used by green belts. It is the roadmap to be used on all projects and process improvements, with the Six Sigma tools applied as needed.

D: Define   This is the overall problem definition step. This definition should be as specific and complete as possible.

M: Measure   Accurate and sufficient measurements and data are needed. Data are the essence of many Six Sigma projects.

A: Analyze   The measurements and data must be analyzed to see if they are consistent with the problem definition and also to see if they identify a root cause. A problem solution is then identified. Sometimes, based on the analysis, it is necessary to go back and restate the problem definition and start the process over.

I: Improve   Once a solution is identified, it must be implemented. After the solution has been implemented, the results must be verified with independent data. Past data are seldom sufficient.

C: Control   A verification of control must be implemented. A robust solution (like a part change) will be easier to keep in control than a qualitative solution.

As we learn to use each tool in the following chapters, we will refer back to its use in the DMAIC process.

D: DEFINE

A problem is often initially identified very qualitatively, without much specific detail:

> "The customer is complaining that the quality of the motors has deteriorated."
>
> "The new personnel-attendance software program keeps crashing."
>
> "The losses on grinder 4 seem higher recently."

Before you can even think about possible solutions, you must define the problem in specific terms. Only then can meaningful measurements or data be collected. Here are the above examples with some additional definition:

> "More of the quarter-horsepower motors are failing the loading test beginning March 20."
>
> "The personnel-attendance software crashes several times per day when the number of absences exceeds 50."
>
> "The incidence of grinder 4 product being scrapped for small diameters has doubled in the last week."

If there were quantitative values available, like the specific change in the number of quarter-horsepower motors failing the loading test, they would be included in the problem definition. The more specific the initial problem definition, the better.

To arrive at a good problem definition may be as simple as talking to the customer. This book provides several excellent tools for quantifying customer input. Often, however, improving the definition will require more effort. Some preliminary measurements may have to be taken to be sure that there even *is* a problem. It may be necessary to verify measurements and calculate sample sizes to be sure that you have valid and sufficient data. Sometimes the resultant measurements and analysis will show that the initial problem definition was erroneous, and you then have to formulate another problem definition.

M: MEASURE

Once the problem has been defined, it must be decided what additional measurements must be taken to quantify it. This book will discuss several tools that help in identifying the key process input variables to be considered and/or measured.

Also, samples used in this step must be sufficient in number, random, and representative of the process you wish to measure.

A: ANALYZE

Now we have to see what the data are telling us. We have to plot the data to understand the process character. We must decide if the problem as defined is real or just a random event without an assignable cause. If the event is random, we cannot look for a specific process change. Our analysis may show that we have to measure additional related key process input variables. The data we gather will also be the base against which we will measure the success of any improvement.

I: IMPROVE

Once we understand the root cause of the problem and have quantitative data, we identify possible solutions. Tests may be required to understand any interaction between the input variables. Tolerances have to be examined to see if they truly represent need.

Once we have tested the possible solutions, we implement the best of those solutions and verify that the results we predicted are actually occurring.

C: CONTROL

Quality control data samples and measurement verification should be scheduled. Updated tolerances should reflect any change.

USING DMAIC

It is strongly recommended that all DMAIC steps be followed when problem solving. It is especially important that you do not make major process changes without doing all the DMAIC steps. Remember, trying to fix a change that was implemented without first working through all the applicable steps may cause you to spend more time responding to the resultant problems than you would have spent if you had taken the time to do it right! It is always tempting to skip steps early in a project to save a little time; but almost always this time savings is small compared to the time required at the end of a project to fix resultant mistakes.

The DMAIC roadmap is not only useful for problem troubleshooting; it also works well as a checklist for doing any other type of project. In addition to any program management tool that is being used to run a project, it is often beneficial to make a list of Six Sigma tools that are planned for use in each stage of the DMAIC process as the project progresses. A Six Sigma tool check-off list should be regularly reviewed and updated as the project progresses.

Case Study: Using the DMAIC Process on a Multiple-Plant Project

A home office engineering team has been using the DMAIC process on all their projects for several years. Since adopting this process, not only has the team's project performance improved but also their customer plants have realized that they are a part of the project process. The customer plants became involved because many Six Sigma tools require input from customers. Using these tools means that even when there are temporary issues, all project participants, including the customers, feel that they are part of the problem and therefore accept that they should be part of the solution.

At the start of every project the engineering team reviews the DMAIC process and develops a list of Six Sigma tools appropriate to the program. At every program meeting this Six Sigma tool check-off list is reviewed to make sure that every element is being followed. There are no surprises. The DMAIC process minimizes the panic and catch-up that often accompanies projects before Six Sigma is applied to them.

The advantage of creating a Six Sigma tool check-off list at the start of a project is that the list makes it less likely that a specific tool will not be used. In the middle of a project, when all sorts of things are happening, including the pressure of other projects, it is easy to skip a tool. That is less likely to happen when you know that the tool is already on a review list against which everyone's performance will be measured.

On a project that was recently completed, the engineering team was in the last step of introducing a new process into four plants that had similar production lines. In each plant there was a specific series of tests that were to be run to verify that each plant's process input variables would be optimized. Several Six Sigma tools were to be used in these tests. These tests required that production be shut down for several days.

After completing these tests in three plants, the plant manager of the fourth plant wanted to skip the process optimization steps because he knew that the input settings in the other plants had all turned out to be identical, and he was confident that his plant would find that the same settings applied. By skipping these tests and just using the same settings, the fourth plant would be able to produce product for two extra days, and the plant would be able to beat their quarterly production target.

The engineering team insisted that the fourth plant run the optimization test as planned, even though they agreed that there was a high likelihood that the input settings would end up being the same as those in the other three plants. At the beginning of the project a Six Sigma check-off list had been developed, and everyone had agreed to do the identified tests in *every* plant because, although the production lines were similar, they were not identical. Representatives from the fourth plant had been part of that decision process, so after reconsideration, they reluctantly agreed to run the planned tests.

The optimization tests were run, and the results revealed that this fourth plant required substantially different input variable settings. Their production line, although having only minor differences, acted quite differently than the lines in the other plants.

Although the fourth plant did not get the additional unplanned production days they had wanted, they got a process that was approximately 2 percent better than what they would have had at the input settings used by the other three plants. This more than compensated for their losing the two extra days of production.

CHAPTER 5 REVIEW

1. The define, measure, analyze, improve, and control (DMAIC) process is the procedural roadmap Six Sigma green belts use to solve problems.

2. The Six Sigma tools are used in different steps in the DMAIC process. The project or problem dictates which tools are used and where in the DMAIC process.

3. The DMAIC process not only is useful as a problem-solving guide but it also can be used as a standardized project format. A Six Sigma tool check-off list is an effective way to make sure applicable tools are identified and used.

4. The use of Six Sigma—both the DMAIC process and the Six Sigma tools—ensures involvement and buy-in from both customers and management.

5. There is less panic and more control when the DMAIC format is followed. Effectiveness improves measurably, as do job satisfaction and reward.

Nonstatistical Six Sigma Tools

Audiatur et altera pars.   (The other part should be heard too.)

—Latin saying

Part Two, which includes Chapters 6 through 11, requires no statistics but includes very powerful Six Sigma tools. Even using these rather simple tools will generate many Six Sigma benefits.

The first two discussed—*quality function deployments* (QFDs) and *failure modes and effects analyses* (FMEAs)—are the primary tools for customer input into the evaluation process. They increase the probability of Six Sigma project success and encourage buy-in.

The next three tools are the *fishbone diagram, process flow diagram,* and *visual correlation checks.* These tools are valuable in identifying the key process input variables and in narrowing the focus when looking for a problem cause.

Chapter 11 emphasizes that tolerances should be reality based. This check of tolerances is technically not a Six Sigma tool, but verifying tolerances is required in many Six Sigma projects.

CHAPTER 6

Simplified QFDs

What you will learn in this chapter is that what a customer really needs is often not truly understood during the design or change of a product, process, or service. Those doing a project often just *assume* that they understand the customer's wants and needs. A simplified QFD will minimize issues arising from this potential lack of understanding.

QFD originally stood for *quality function deployment*. Years ago, when quality departments were generally much larger, quality engineers were "deployed" to customers to rigorously probe the customers' needs. The engineers then created a series of forms that transitioned those needs into a set of actions for the supplier. The simplified QFD attempts to accomplish the same task in a condensed manner.

If you were limited to only one Six Sigma tool, you would use the simplified QFD. It is useable on any type of problem, and it *should* be used on *every* problem. It takes a relatively small amount of time and gets much buy-in from customers. QFDs don't always get the respect they deserve because they don't look complex. But they are a very powerful tool!

What is presented here is a simplified version of the QFDs likely to be presented in many Six Sigma classes. Some descriptions of the traditional QFDs and the rationale for the simplification will be given later in this chapter. The simplified QFD is usually used in the Define or Improve steps of the DMAIC process.

A simplified QFD does not require any statistics. But it is usually necessary to do a simplified QFD to understand what actions are needed to address a problem or implement a project. The specific actions that are identified in the QFD or in any of the other qualitative tools are often what trigger the application of the statistically based Six Sigma tools.

Many product, process, and service issues are caused by not incorporating input from customers and/or suppliers of

---

Simplified QFDs

The simplified QFD converts customer needs into prioritized actions, which can then be addressed as individual projects. Here are some examples of how a QFD is used.

Manufacturing
Use the simplified QFD to get customer input as to their needs at the start of every new design or before any change in process or equipment.

New Product Development
Simplified QFDs are very effective in transitioning and prioritizing customer wants into specific items to be incorporated into a new product.

Sales and Marketing
Before any new sales initiative, do a simplified QFD, inviting potential customers, salespeople, advertisement suppliers, and others to give input.

Accounting and Software Development
Before developing a new program language or software package, do a simplified QFD. A customer's input will be essential for a seamless implementation of the program.

Receivables
Do a simplified QFD on whether your approach on collecting receivables is optimal. Besides those directly involved in dealing with collectables, invite customers who are overdue on receivables to participate (you may have to give them some debt relief to get their cooperation).

Insurance
Do a simplified QFD with customers to see what they look for in an insurance company or what it would take to make them switch.

components and raw materials early in a design or process change. Even if the manufacturer, supplier, designer, or service department *does* know what customers need, it is always advisable to have the customers be part of any decision process so they know that their input has been considered.

The "customers" in this case include everyone who will touch the product while or after it is made, such as suppliers, production, packaging, shipping, sales, and the end users. They are all influenced by any design or process change. Operators of equipment, service people, and implementers can be both customers and suppliers.

The most important (and often the most difficult) step in doing any QFD is getting the suppliers, operators, and customers together to fill out the required QFD form. Nevertheless, every group affected by the project should be represented. The desires of one group will sometimes cause limitations on others, but on the other hand, simultaneous discussions among the factions will often bring to light some options not previously considered, which will give the working group the opportunity to identify the best possible overall solution. As you read the following details, refer to the simplified QFD form in Figure 6–1 to see the application.

INSTRUCTIONS FOR SIMPLIFIED QFDs

The simplified QFD form provides a way of quantifying design options, always measuring these options against customer needs. The first step in doing the simplified QFD form is to make a list of the customer needs, with each need being rated with a value of from 1 to 5:

5 is a critical or a safety need, a need that must be satisfied.
4 is very important.
3 is highly desirable.
2 is nice to have.
1 is wanted if it's easy to do.

You can use a more elaborate rating system, with more numerical steps, but if you do that, you will find you spend too much time assigning numbers! Also, don't let a disagreement between a

F I G U R E   6–1

Example of a Simplified QFD Form

		Design Items									

QFD: License Plate Holder Option for Luxury Automobile

Ratings: 5 highest to 1 lowest (or negative number).
Numbers in parentheses are the result of multiplying
the customer need rating by the design item rating.

Customer Needs	Ratings	Metal Cast Rim	Plastic Cast Complete	Stamped Steel Rim	All Holes Already In	Optional Punched Holes	Gold/Silver Plating	Hex/Slotted Plastic Screws	Hex/Slotted Plated Steel Screws	Plastic Lens, Separate	Tempered-Glass Lens, Separate
Embossed Name	5	5 (25)	5 (25)	3 (15)	0 (0)	0 (0)	0 (0)	0 (0)	0 (0)	0 (0)	0 (0)
Place for Dealer Name	5	5 (25)	5 (25)	5 (25)	0 (0)	0 (0)	0 (0)	0 (0)	0 (0)	0 (0)	0 (0)
Must Hold All State Plates	5	5 (25)	5 (25)	5 (25)	5 (25)	5 (25)	0 (0)	0 (0)	0 (0)	0 (0)	0 (0)
Solid Feel	3	5 (15)	3 (9)	2 (6)	0 (0)	0 (0)	0 (0)	1 (3)	4 (12)	2 (6)	5 (15)
Gold or Silver Option	2	5 (10)	5 (10)	3 (6)	0 (0)	0 (0)	5 (10)	5 (10)	5 (10)	0 (0)	0 (0)
Easy to Install	4	3 (12)	5 (20)	3 (12)	5 (20)	3 (12)	0 (0)	5 (20)	3 (12)	3 (12)	2 (8)
Corrosion Resistant	4	3 (12)	5 (20)	2 (8)	0 (0)	0 (0)	3 (12)	5 (20)	3 (12)	4 (16)	5 (20)
Light Weight (for MPG)	1	1 (1)	4 (4)	5 (5)	0 (0)	0 (0)	0 (0)	5 (5)	2 (2)	5 (5)	1 (1)
Luxury Look	4	5 (20)	2 (8)	1 (4)	2 (8)	4 (16)	5 (20)	1 (4)	5 (20)	2 (8)	5 (20)
No Sharp Corners	5	4 (20)	5 (25)	2 (10)	4 (20)	2 (10)	0 (0)	5 (25)	3 (15)	5 (25)	2 (10)
Transparent Lens	4	0 (0)	3 (12)	0 (0)	0 (0)	0 (0)	0 (0)	0 (0)	0 (0)	3 (12)	5 (20)
Last 10 Years	5	4 (20)	4 (20)	3 (15)	0 (0)	0 (0)	3 (15)	5 (25)	4 (20)	3 (15)	5 (25)
Low Cost	2	1 (2)	5 (10)	4 (8)	5 (10)	2 (4)	1 (2)	5 (10)	3 (6)	4 (8)	2 (4)
Keep Appearance 10 Years	4	4 (16)	3 (12)	2 (8)	0 (0)	0 (0)	2 (8)	5 (20)	3 (12)	3 (12)	5 (20)
GROUPINGS **TOTALS** **PRIORITIES**		(203)	(225)	(147)	(83)	(67)	(67)	(142)	(121)	(119)	(143)
			1		3		4	2		NA	NA

3 and a 4 disrupt the meeting. Just pick one. However, any large disagreement in the group as to what the rating on an item should be should trigger a discussion. This disagreement is a hint that there is some misunderstanding as to what the customer need really is or its importance. The customer needs and ratings are listed down the left-hand side of the simplified QFD form.

Across the top of the simplified QFD form are potential actions to address the customer needs. Note that the customer needs are often expressed qualitatively (easy to use, won't rust, long life, etc.), whereas the design action items listed will be more specific (tabulated input screen, stainless steel, sealed roller bearings, etc.). Under each design action item and opposite each customer need, insert a value (1 to 5) to rate how strongly that design item addresses the customer need:

5 means it addresses the customer need completely.

4 means it addresses the customer need well.

3 means it addresses the customer need some.

2 means it addresses the customer need a little.

1 means it addresses the customer need very little.

0 or blank means it does not affect the customer need.

A negative number means it is detrimental to that customer need. (A negative number is not that unusual since a solution to one need sometimes subtracts from another need!)

Put the rating in the upper half of the block beneath the design item and opposite the need. Then multiply the design rating times the value assigned to the corresponding customer need value. Enter this result into the lower half of the square under the design action item rating. These values will have a possible range of a -25 to $+25$ and are shown in parentheses in Figure 6–1.

Once all the design items are rated against every customer need, the values in the lower half of the boxes (in parentheses) under each design item are summed and entered into the totals row at the bottom of the sheet. The solutions with the highest values are usually the preferred design solutions to address the customer needs.

Once these totals are reviewed, someone may feel that something is awry and want to go back and review some ratings or design solutions. This second (or third) review is extremely valuable. Also, the customer 5 ratings should be discussed one at a time to make sure that they are being addressed sufficiently.

Both the identification of customer needs and potential actions to address these needs may require some brainstorming. One of the tools that can assist in this brainstorming is the fishbone diagram, which is discussed in Chapter 8. Also, sometimes the list of potential actions to address the customer's needs is best done at a second meeting, after people have had some time to digest the list of customer needs.

Figure 6–1 is an example of a simplified QFD. The simplified QFD form can be done by hand or in *Excel*. In either case, the list building and item rating should be done "live" in the meeting so that the QFD will benefit from the maximum amount of interaction and participation possible.

Note that the QFDs shown in this book are a lot neater and more organized than they would appear in the live meetings where the QFDs are being developed. During the meetings, the needs and potential actions may not be logically grouped or necessarily in prioritized order. A more organized QFD, as shown in Figure 6–1, will occur later, when it is formalized.

In the simplified QFD form, near the bottom, design action items are grouped when only one of several options can be done. In this case there would be only one priority number assigned to the highest valued design action item within the group.

In the case presented in Figure 6–1, the priorities showed that the supplier should cast a plastic license plate cover with built-in plastic lens. This would preclude the need for a separate lens, which is why the NA (not applicable) is shown in the separate lens grouping. The unit would be mounted using plastic screws, with holes for all plates cast in. Gold or silver plating was an option that could be applied to the rim of the plastic. Note that some of the luxury items (like steel casting) weren't picked because other factors were deemed more important.

Having the customers be present for discussions like the one illustrated by Figure 6–1 is critical so that they will not feel that the supplier is giving them something other than what they really want. Often customers will start out with a wish list that is then trimmed down to a few critical items.

The simplified QFD form should be completed for all new designs or process modifications. The form itself can be tweaked to make it more applicable to the product, process, or service it is addressing.

The most important part of the QFD process is getting involvement from as many affected parties as possible and incorporating their input into the simplified QFD form so that it can be used to influence design direction. The time and/or cost involved in having the required meetings will be more than offset by having correct design decisions made up front, which is much better than having to fix design errors later.

Case Study: Options for Repairing a High-Speed Machine

A high-speed production machine had a large number of molds that opened and closed as they traveled along the process. At one location in the molds' journey, the molds would contact the product after it was produced, at times causing a mark in that product. This contact was caused by wear in the mechanism that carried the molds, which allowed the molds to have excess play. The manufacturing plant wanted to see if there was a way to eliminate this problem without a complete rebuilding of the mechanism that carried the molds. The complete rebuild was a known baseline option if no better solution was identified. Figure 6–2 is the QFD that was done on this issue.

One of the engineers at the QFD meeting came up with a seemingly clever idea to use magnets to hold the molds open at the problem area on the machine, where the molds were contacting the product. This was the chosen option, which was far less expensive than the baseline approach of a rebuild.

This idea was then modeled in a laboratory, using actual molds and various strength magnets that were already on hand. Everything that was seen in the tests exceeded expectations. Different distances between the molds and magnets were tested, and the distance was not critical. Nor was the speed of the molds as they went by the magnets. As long as the magnets were relatively strong, their strength was also not critical.

Engineers from the production plant were invited to view the tests, and they became very enthused. They also saw no issues. Once they reported back to their plant, we began to get calls from the plant manager asking us when we could try this on the actual production machine.

We explained that, per the Six Sigma roadmap, there was one more meeting we had to have with the plant people, and if there were no unexpected issues that came up in that meeting, we would then go ahead and schedule a production machine test.

This project is discussed further in the next chapter on FMEAs.

F I G U R E 6–2

Machine Repair Options QFD

Ratings: 5 highest to 1 lowest (or negative number).
Numbers in parentheses are the result of multiplying
the customer need rating by the design item rating.

Customer Needs	Ratings	Rebuild Current Design	Rebuild Lighter Design	Increase Cam Opening Distance	Machine-Off Mold Contact Area	Use Air to Hold Molds	Use Vacuum to Hold Molds	Use Magnets to Hold Molds
				Design Items				
Inexpensive	4	2	1	3	4	3	2	5
		(8)	(4)	(12)	(16)	(12)	(8)	(20)
Quick	2	2	1	3	3	5	2	5
		(4)	(2)	(6)	(6)	(10)	(4)	(10)
Low Risk	4	5	4	1	1	1	0	5
		(20)	(16)	(4)	(4)	(4)	(0)	(20)
Quality OK	5	5	5	1	1	1	4	5
		(25)	(25)	(5)	(5)	(5)	(20)	(25)
Permanent Fix	3	4	5	1	1	3	3	5
		(12)	(15)	(3)	(3)	(9)	(9)	(15)
Easy	2	2	1	2	4	3	4	5
		(4)	(2)	(4)	(8)	(6)	(8)	(10)
Little Downtime	3	2	1	3	4	4	4	5
		(6)	(3)	(9)	(12)	(12)	(12)	(15)
TOTALS		(79)	(67)	(43)	(54)	(58)	(61)	(115)
PRIORITIES		2	3					1

Case Study: A Simplified QFD to Help Sell Art

To show how versatile this tool is, about a year ago an artist friend asked me if Six Sigma could help her sell additional art and help her sell her art for more money. She wanted to make a full-time living as an artist. Most people think that her art is quite good, so the assumption was that some other problem was hindering her from being a successful full-time artist. I decided that a QFD might help identify the customer "wants" on art and see if she was doing the right kind of art to make a living.

Besides the artist, three other people—an art agent, a high-end gallery manager, and a successful full-time artist—agreed to contribute to a QFD on the subject.

The team decided to look at the question three different ways: art subject, art medium, and art sales method. In Chapter 8 on fishbone diagrams you will see how the inputs for this QFD were identified. Figures 6–3 through 6–5 show the results of the three elements of this QFD.

FIGURE 6–3

Art Subject

Ratings: 5 highest to 1 lowest (or negative number).
Numbers in parentheses are the result of multiplying
the customer need rating by the artist item rating.

Customer Needs on Expensive ($500+) Originals	Ratings	Personal Portrait	Generic Portrait	Landscape	Nude Defined	Nude Subtle	Modern Nonreal
				Artist Items			
Perceived Quality	5	3 (15)	3 (15)	3 (15)	3 (15)	3 (15)	3 (15)
Acceptable Home or Office	5	3 (15)	3 (15)	5 (25)	1 (5)	3 (15)	3 (15)
Attractive to Buyer	3	4 (12)	3 (9)	3 (9)	2 (6)	3 (9)	2 (6)
Enhance Home or Office	4	3 (12)	2 (8)	3 (12)	1 (4)	2 (8)	2 (8)
Somewhat Unique	2	5 (10)	2 (4)	3 (6)	3 (6)	4 (8)	2 (4)
Compatible Colors	3	3 (9)	3 (9)	3 (9)	3 (9)	3 (9)	2 (6)
Attractive to Friends	5	3 (15)	1 (5)	3 (15)	1 (5)	2 (10)	1 (5)
Status Symbol	5	5 (25)	1 (5)	3 (15)	3 (15)	3 (15)	1 (5)
Conversation Piece	3	5 (15)	3 (9)	3 (9)	3 (9)	4 (12)	2 (6)
Artist Is Not an Amateur	4	(0)	(0)	(0)	3 (12)	3 (12)	(0)
Permanence or Substance	4	3 (12)	3 (12)	3 (12)	3 (12)	3 (12)	3 (12)
Last Many Generations	5	5 (25)	(0)	2 (10)	(0)	2 (10)	1 (5)
Perceived Cultural	5	5 (25)	3 (15)	3 (15)	2 (10)	3 (15)	2 (10)
TOTALS		(190)	(106)	(152)	(108)	(150)	(97)
PRIORITIES		1		2			

FIGURE 6—4

Art Medium

Ratings: 5 highest to 1 lowest (or negative number).
Numbers in parentheses are the result of multiplying
the customer need rating by the artist item rating.

Customer Needs on Expensive ($500+) Originals	Ratings	Oil	Watercolor	Acrylic	Pencil, Charcoal, Pastel
Perceived Quality	5	5 (25)	4 (20)	2 (10)	2 (10)
Acceptable Home or Office	5	5 (25)	5 (25)	5 (25)	5 (25)
Attractive to Buyer	3	5 (15)	5 (15)	5 (15)	5 (15)
Enhance Home or Office	4	5 (20)	5 (20)	5 (20)	5 (20)
Somewhat Unique	2	3 (6)	3 (6)	2 (4)	2 (4)
Compatible Colors	3	3 (9)	3 (9)	3 (9)	2 (6)
Attractive to Friends	5	3 (15)	3 (15)	2 (10)	2 (10)
Status Symbol	5	4 (20)	4 (20)	2 (10)	2 (10)
Conversation Piece	3	4 (12)	4 (12)	2 (6)	2 (6)
Artist Is Not an Amateur	4	4 (16)	3 (12)	2 (8)	2 (8)
Permanence or Substance	4	5 (20)	4 (16)	3 (12)	2 (8)
Last Many Generations	5	5 (25)	4 (20)	3 (15)	2 (10)
Perceived Cultural	5	5 (25)	5 (25)	3 (15)	3 (15)
TOTALS		(233)	(215)	(159)	(147)
PRIORITIES		1	2		

FIGURE 6—5

Art Sales Method

Customer Needs on Expensive ($500+) Originals	Ratings	High-End Gallery/Agent	Prestige Show	Local Show
Ratings: 5 highest to 1 lowest (or negative number). Numbers in parentheses are the result of multiplying the customer need rating by the artist item rating.		**Artist Items**		
Perceived Quality	5	5 (25)	4 (20)	2 (10)
Acceptable Home or Office	5	5 (25)	4 (20)	2 (10)
Attractive to Buyer	3			
Enhance Home or Office	4			
Somewhat Unique	2			
Compatible Colors	3			
Attractive to Friends	5	4 (20)	2 (10)	(0)
Status Symbol	5	5 (25)	4 (20)	2 (10)
Conversation Piece	3	5 (15)	4 (12)	3 (9)
Artist Is Not an Amateur	4	5 (20)	4 (16)	2 (8)
Permanence or Substance	4	5 (20)	4 (16)	(0)
Last Many Generations	5	5 (25)	4 (20)	2 (10)
Perceived Cultural	5	5 (25)	4 (20)	2 (10)
TOTALS		(200)	(154)	(67)
PRIORITIES		1	2	

The results of the QFDs showed that the artist should be painting personal portraits; they should be painted in oil and then sold either through a high-end gallery or an agent. This was *not* what the artist was doing. She belonged to an artists' group that met weekly and painted live models, both portraits and nudes, and she was painting or drawing whatever she wanted to paint or draw. She often used charcoal, pastel (chalk), or even pencil. Her paintings (or drawings) were excellent, and she would display them for sale at public places such as local shows and restaurants. She did not want to pay the 40 percent that galleries or agents normally charge for selling art. She sold little art.

Once she started making and selling art based on the QFD finding, her art began to be in demand, and she could charge more, easily overcoming the 40 percent she had to pay an agent.

Case Study: A Simplified QFD on a Test Cutting Machine

A simplified QFD was being done to determine what adjustments were to be incorporated on a test inline cutting machine for extruded tubing. The intent of this project was to instrument a cutting machine sufficiently to test all reasonable combinations of settings to identify an optimum cutting process. The existing cutting machines would, when cutting the tubing, leave a rough end on the tube. This caused excessive material losses.

Future production machines would be designed with features dictated by the results found using the test cutting machine. The simplified QFD was to identify what items were to be tested on this test inline cutter. Then equipment design engineers would have to design that test capability into the test machine.

In attendance at this simplified QFD meeting was a Ph.D. who had studied the process, equipment design and process engineers, customers who emphasized what issues had to be addressed, and some operators and maintenance people knowledgeable of the current cutting equipment.

The machine operators were quiet until the end of the meeting, when they became insistent that an additional support spring be added. None of the "experts" felt that this additional support spring was needed, and they opposed adding it because the operators could not logically explain the rationale for the spring. The operators' experience, however, made them adamant that the support spring was needed. Since the operators were so insistent and the worst thing that would happen is that the added spring would prove to be not needed, it was decided to include the additional support spring against the advice of the academic "experts."

When the test was run to find the optimum settings, it was found that this additional support spring was critical. The cutting process was very unstable without this support spring being optimized. Without the simplified QFD, this spring would not have been incorporated and the process optimization would not have been successful.

The knowledge gained from this piece of test equipment was incorporated into the design of 12 inline extruded tubing cutters, saving $1,500,000 per year.

THE EDSEL CONCERN

In 1958 the Ford Motor Company marketed a new automobile called the *Edsel*. This car was introduced with much fanfare because its design was dictated by many in-depth surveys on consumers' wants. However, the final design was considered a disaster, and it became a laughing stock with its incongruous design features.

For those just being introduced to QFDs, the prior Edsel disaster is often a concern. A similar concern is expressed well in the oft-stated observation that a camel is a horse designed by a committee. The concern related to QFDs is that input from a diverse group of people will cause a product to be designed, or a process to be changed, without resultant design or logic synergy.

The differences between the QFD approach and the above examples are that when doing a QFD the final design or project responsibility is not switched to the customer or even to the QFD team. It is the *inputs* from a balanced team of knowledgeable people that are needed, not a final design or change decision responsibility. The final project, process, or design decision responsibility does not change; the input just makes those decision makers more knowledgeable. That is why it is emphasized that the priorities identified at the bottom of the QFD form are *often, but not always*, the specific actions to be taken. The identified priorities should not overrule other concerns like physics, safety, and design congruity.

TRADITIONAL QFDs

A traditional QFD, as taught in most classes on Six Sigma, is likely to make use of one of the following formats.

The first and most likely is a QFD consisting of four forms. The first form in this QFD is the "House of Quality." This form covers product planning and competitor benchmarking. The second form is "Part Deployment," which shows key part characteristics. The third form shows "Critical-to-Customer Process Operations." The fourth is "Production Planning."

Two other possible QFDs are the "Matrix of Matrices," consisting of 30 matrices, and the "Designer's Dozen," consisting of 12 matrices.

Needless to say, these other QFDs take much more time and effort than the simplified QFD. Meetings to complete the traditional QFDs generally take at least four times as long as the meetings required for the simplified QFD on an equivalent project.

Are the traditional QFDs worth the extra effort versus the simplified QFD? Perhaps on very large and very complex programs. However, the benefit of being able to use the simplified QFD on *every* project or change, which is not realistic for the more complex QFDs, gives it a decided advantage. The customers' inputs are needed on *all* levels of projects!

The major benefit of any QFD comes from getting the input of everyone affected. If the form is too complex, or the meeting to do the form is too long, people lose focus, their eyes begin to blur, and the quality of the input diminishes. Often people in traditional QFD meetings find reasons they have to leave early or find excuses not to come in the first place. The simplified QFD is designed to get needed input with the minimum of hassle. Simplified QFD meetings are often only two or three hours long.

CHAPTER 6 REVIEW

1. The simplified QFD is usually used in the Define or Improve steps of the DMAIC process.

2. Many product, process, and service issues are caused by not incorporating input from customers and/or suppliers of components and raw materials early in a design or process change. Often the manufacturer just assumes that what the customer really wants is already known.

3. The use of a simplified QFD can minimize a lot of issues before a design or modification is implemented.

4. Everyone affected by the project—such as operators, suppliers, users, engineering, maintenance, and customers—must participate in generating the simplified QFD form.

5. The simplified QFD should be done as early in a project as possible.

6. The simplified QFD's priority results should be revisited several times to make sure that they truly reflect the group's intent.

7. The cost of doing a simplified QFD will be more than offset by the benefits of a superior design, with fewer modifications required.

8. The simplified QFD should be used on *every* new product and on every product or process change.

9. There are more complex and detailed QFDs that may be worth considering for use on very large and complex programs. However, the effort and people required for these QFDs usually preclude their being used on *all* designs and changes. The simplified QFD is extremely practical since it *can* be used be used on *all* designs and changes.

Simplified FMEAs

What we will learn in this chapter is that on any project there can be collateral damage to areas outside it, but simplified *failure modes and effects analysis* (FMEA) will reduce this likelihood. A simplified FMEA will generate savings largely through cost avoidance. It is usually used in the Define or Improve steps of the DMAIC process.

A simplified FMEA is used in conjunction with the simplified QFD. It is the opposite side of the same coin, and it is equally important. Both Six Sigma tools should be used on every project or process change and on any new development.

As was true for simplified QFDs, as presented in Chapter 6, the simplified FMEA will be less complex than the FMEA taught in most Six Sigma classes. A brief discussion of the traditional FMEA and the reason for the simplification comes later in the chapter.

Note that the simplified FMEA format is very similar to that used for the simplified QFD. This is intentional, since the goal is to use *both* on *every* new product or change. Since many of the same people will be working on both the QFD and the FMEA, the commonality of the two forms simplifies the task.

A simplified FMEA is a method for anticipating things that can go wrong even if a proposed project, task, or modification is completed as expected. Often a project generates so much support and enthusiasm that it lacks a healthy amount of skeptics,

---

The Simplified FMEA

The simplified FMEA uses input on concerns to address collateral risks. The following examples illustrate different ways an FMEA can be used to further project goals.

Manufacturing
Before implementing any new design, process, or change, do a simplified FMEA. An FMEA converts qualitative concerns into specific actions. You need input on what possible negative effects could occur.

Sales and Marketing
A change in a sales or marketing strategy can affect other products or cause an aggressive response by a competitor. A simplified FMEA is one way to make sure that all the possible ramifications are understood.

Accounting and Software Development
The introduction of a new software package or a different accounting procedure sometimes causes unexpected problems for those affected. A simplified FMEA will reduce unforeseen problems.

Receivables
How receivables are handled can affect future sales with a customer. A simplified FMEA will help to highlight the concerns of both the customer and internal salespeople and identify approaches that minimize future sales risks while reducing overdue receivables.

Insurance
The balance between profits and servicing customers on insurance claims is dynamic. A simplified FMEA helps keep people attuned to risks associated with any action under consideration.

---

especially in regards to any effects that project may have on things not directly related to the project. Everyone's effort is on getting the project going, and little effort is spent on looking at ramifications beyond the specific project task. There are usually multiple ways to solve a problem, and the best solution is often the one that has the least risk to other parts of the process.

The simplified FMEA form is a way of giving a project a critical look before it is implemented, so it often saves a lot of cost and embarrassment. In doing a simplified FMEA, it is assumed that all inherent components of the direct project will be done correctly. (They should have been covered in regular project reviews.) The emphasis in a simplified FMEA is to identify affected components or issues downstream, or on tangentially related processes that may have issues caused by the program.

Just as in the simplified QFD, the critical step is getting everyone together who has anything to do with the project, especially those having to deal with the effect of the project. These people could be machine operators, customers, shipping personnel, or even suppliers. The proper group of participants will vary per project.

INSTRUCTIONS FOR SIMPLIFIED FMEAs

The left-hand column of the simplified FMEA form (see Figure 7–1) is a list of possible things that could go wrong, assuming that the project is completed as planned. The first task of the meeting is to generate this list of concerns. On this list could be unforeseen issues on other parts of the process, safety issues, environmental concerns, negative effects on existing similar products, or even employee problems. These will be rated in importance:

5 is a safety or critical concern.

4 is a very important concern.

3 is a medium concern.

2 is a minor concern.

1 is a matter for discussion to see if it is an issue.

Across the top of the simplified FMEA is a list of solutions already in place to address the concerns or additional potential solutions that have been identified in the meeting. Below each potential solution and opposite the concern, each response item is rated on how well it addresses the concern:

5 means it addresses the concern completely.

4 means it addresses the concern well.

3 means it addresses the concern satisfactorily.

2 means it addresses the concern somewhat.

1 means it addresses the concern very little.

0 or a blank means it does not affect the concern.

A negative number means the solution actually makes that concern worse.

Enter this value in the upper half of the block, beneath the solution item and opposite the concern. After these ratings are completed, multiply each rating times the concern value on the left. Enter this product in the lower half of each box. Add all the values in the lower half of the boxes in each column, and enter the sum in the totals row indicated near the bottom of the form. These are then prioritized, with the highest value being the No. 1 consideration for implementation.

As in the simplified QFD, these summations are only a point of reference. It is appropriate to reexamine the concerns and ratings.

The subject for the following case study was already covered in Chapter 6, where a QFD was developed.

Case Study: A Potentially Lifesaving, Simplified FMEA on Repairing a High-Speed Machine

A high-speed production machine was experiencing wear issues. This wear caused the tooling to have too much play, which allowed it to rub against the product at one specific location on the machine, causing quality issues. The cost of rebuilding the machine was very high, so the manufacturing plant wanted other options for solving this problem.

An engineer came up with what seemed like an ingenious solution. Powerful magnets would be mounted just outboard of the machine at the problem area, near the steel tooling. These magnets would attract and hold open the steel tooling as it went by, moving the tooling away from the product and eliminating the chance of the tooling rubbing against the product. This solution was especially attractive because it would be inexpensive and easy to do and it would solve the problem completely. The initial engineering study found no showstoppers in regard to installing the magnets. Bench tests with actual magnets and tooling indicated that it would work extremely well.

Everyone was anxious to implement this solution since all the parts were readily available and they would be easy to install on the machine for a test. But a requirement of the Six Sigma process was to first do a simplified FMEA to see if this solution could cause other issues. So a group of production engineers, foremen, operators, maintenance people, and quality technicians were invited to a meeting to do the simplified FMEA.

Figure 7–1 is the simplified FMEA as derived in the meeting. Most of the concerns that surfaced had doable and effective solutions. However, the input that one of the machine operators had a heart pacemaker was a complete surprise, and no one had any idea of how the magnets would affect the pacemaker.

On following up with the pacemaker manufacturer, it was discovered that even the pacemaker manufacturer was not sure how their device would be affected by the powerful magnets. They did say, however, that they had serious reservations.

FIGURE 7–1

A Potentially Lifesaving Simplified FMEA

FMEA: Magnets Holding Tooling Open					
Ratings: 5 highest to 1 lowest (or negative number). Numbers in parentheses are the result of multiplying the customer concern rating by the solution item rating.					
		Solutions			
Concerns	Ratings	Mount a Degausser after Magnets	Mount ProxSwitch and Use Breakaway Mounts	Use Electric Magnets; Adjust Current and Turn off to Clean	Check with Pacemaker Mfg: Shield If Required
Tooling Will Become Magetized	4	4 (16)	0 (0)	0 (0)	0 (0)
Caught Product Will Hit Magnets, Wreck Machine	5	0 (0)	3 (15)	0 (0)	0 (0)
Magnets Will Get Covered with Metal Filings	2	2 (4)	0 (0)	3 (6)	0 (0)
One Operator Has a Heart Pacemaker	5	? (?)	0 (0)	0 (0)	? (?)
Magnets Will Cause Violent Tooling Movement	2	0 (0)	0 (0)	3 (6)	0 (0)
TOTALS PRIORITIES		(?)	(15)	(12)	(?)

The pacemaker manufacturer didn't want to commit to what level of shielding would suffice to protect the operator, and they were afraid of any resultant liability. Other sources were researched for guidance, but no other information was found on how the powerful magnets would affect a pacemaker.

The pacemaker manufacturer was not interested in testing one of their pacemakers in their own labs using one of the proposed magnets. They wanted no involvement whatsoever!

Other options were discussed, like reassigning the operator to a different machine, but all of those options raised issues (such as union issues on the reassignment).

The machine operator had to be free to access all areas of the machine, so a barrier physically isolating the area around the magnets was not an option.

At that point the option of using magnets was abandoned because there seemed to be no way to eliminate the possible risk to the operator with the pacemaker. No other low-cost solution was identified. The machine had to be rebuilt despite the high cost.

Without the simplified FMEA the project would have been implemented, with some real risk that the operator could have been hurt or even lost his life.

Although the preceding case study is more dramatic than most, seldom is a simplified FMEA done without uncovering some issue that was previously unknown. Most of these issues can be resolved, and it's easier to resolve them up front than afterward! In this case study the machine was rebuilt. This was the probable outcome in any case; the simplified FMEA prevented the risk, cost, and embarrassment of installing the magnets, dealing with the effects, and removing the magnets.

In the previous chapter on QFDs, there was a case study showing how a QFD was developed to assist an artist in selling art. We have emphasized that both a QFD and an FMEA are to be used on every project or process change. So here is the related FMEA case study for the artwork selling project.

Case Study: A Simplified FMEA on Selling Art

After the simplified QFD was completed and reviewed with the artist, the team was asked to do an FMEA. The artist didn't see the need, but the agent, gallery owner, and other artist were supportive so we proceeded. Figure 7–2 shows the FMEA that the team developed.

The reason that "art won't sell even with changes" was a concern is because even though this artist had shown much skill in her current art, that didn't mean that she had the required skills to make oil portraits that are attractive to high-end buyers. There is a fine line between making a portrait look like someone and making it complimentary to the buyer. Not every artist can walk that line. Even if they *can* walk that line, some artists get bored by the constraints. Also, doing personal portraits requires travel and interface with the customers, who are sometimes very fixed and demanding in their expectations.

The three highest-ranking potential ways to address the concerns identified on the FMEA were, first, for the artist to keep her current job rather than risking everything in the hope that her art would sell sufficiently to support her full time. Second, the artist should remain active with the art group so she would still have diversity in her art. Third, she should offer several styles of portraits (head only, full figure, standing, sitting, etc.), for diversity. The artist is currently successfully doing these three things.

F I G U R E   7–2

Simplified FMEA
Adjust Art to Maximize Sales

Ratings: 5 highest to 1 lowest (or negative number). Numbers in parentheses are the result of multiplying the customer concern rating by the solution item rating.						
		Solutions				
Concerns	Ratings	Don't Quit Day Job	Stay with Art Group	Offer Optional Stylized Portraits	Use Photos, Not Live	Limit Geography (Use Gallery, Not Agent)
Art Won't Sell Even with Changes	4	5 (20)	0 (0)	2 (8)	0 (0)	−2 (−8)
Art Will Become Boring for the Artist	3	1 (3)	5 (15)	5 (15)	0 (0)	0 (0)
Customer Demands Will Be Tiresome	3	2 (6)	3 (9)	0 (0)	3 (9)	0 (0)
Will Require Excessive Travel	1	2 (2)	1 1	0 (0)	2 (2)	4 (4)
Excessive Customer Interface	2	3 (6)	2 (4)	0 (0)	2 (4)	0 (0)
TOTALS		(37)	(29)	(23)	(15)	(−4)
PRIORITIES		1	2	3	4	

TRADITIONAL FMEAs

As mentioned earlier, the simplified FMEA is less complex than the traditional FMEA normally taught in Six Sigma. A traditional FMEA requires the people doing the form to identify each potential failure event, and then for each of these events to identify the failure mode, consequences of a failure, potential cause of the failure, severity of a failure, current design controls to prevent a failure, failure detection likelihood, expected frequency of a failure, impact of the failure, risk priority, recommended action to prevent the failure, and the likelihood of that action succeeding.

This traditional FMEA requires multiple forms and much time to complete.

Is the extra time and effort worth it? As with the traditional QFD, perhaps the additional effort is worthwhile on very complex and large programs. However, since the simplified FMEA takes far less time, it can be used on *every* project or change, which is unlikely to happen with a traditional FMEA. This gives the simplified FMEA a real advantage because collateral damage can occur on *all* levels of project or change.

Both the traditional and simplified FMEAs trigger consideration of collateral damage, so one of the two should be used. Obviously the author prefers the simplified FMEA.

CHAPTER 7 REVIEW

1. A simplified FMEA is usually used in the Define or Improve steps of the DMAIC process.

2. Much effort goes into making sure the specific details of a project, process, or service are correct. However, areas not innately tied to the project are often ignored.

3. A Simplified FMEA emphasizes identifying concerns in other affected areas and prioritizing potential solutions to these concerns.

4. Everyone affected by the proposed project, process, or service should participate in the simplified FMEA.

5. Revisit the results of the simplified FMEA several times to make sure that they truly reflect the group's intent.

6. The cost of doing a simplified FMEA will be more than offset by the costs avoided on the project's potential negative effects on other areas.

7. Traditional FMEAs are more complex, but may be justified on extremely large and complex programs. But they are unlikely to be used on *every* program or change, which is the value of the simplified FMEA.

CHAPTER 8

Fishbone Diagrams

What you will learn in this chapter is that it is critical to identify and examine all the possible causes for a problem. This chapter explains how a fishbone diagram is used to assist in this task.

The fishbone diagram is used primarily in the Define, Analyze, and Improve steps of the DMAIC process. It helps identify which input variables should be studied further and gives focus to the analysis.

Fishbone diagrams, like QFDs and FMEAs, often don't get their due respect because they don't look complex. But they are extremely useful and work well when used in conjunction with QFDs. In fact, sometimes they must be used *before* doing the QFD to assist in generating the list of customer "wants."

Project teams use a fishbone diagram to identify all the input variables that could be causing the problem of interest and then to look for cause-and-effect relationships. Once we have a complete list of input variables, we can identify the critical few key process input variables (KPIVs) to measure and further investigate.

Many of you may have taken part in brainstorming sessions where ideas are put on a board without discussion. The ideas are grouped, voted upon, prioritized, and then the top ones are discussed. The reason for not discussing the ideas earlier is to encourage far-out ideas without critical commentary. Doing a fishbone diagram is different in that active discussion is encouraged every step of the way as the fishbone is being developed. In this way we get synergy in idea generation. We truly want everyone's input on every idea, not just their own. The presumption is that the participants would be sensitive in their comments on others' ideas.

The Fishbone Diagram

Use a fishbone diagram to identify possible key process inputs that may have a cause-and-effect relationship to the problem being studied.

Manufacturing
Do a fishbone diagram to list all the important input variables related to a problem. Highlight the KPIVs for further study. This focus minimizes sample collection and data analysis.

Sales and Marketing
For periods of unusually low sales, use a fishbone diagram to identify possible causes of the low sales. The KPIVs enable identification of probable causes and often lead to possible solutions.

Accounting and Software Development
Use a fishbone diagram to identify the possible causes of unusual accounting or computer issues. The people in these areas respond well to this type of analysis.

Receivables
Identify periods of higher-than-normal delinquent receivables. Then use a fishbone diagram to try and understand the underlying causes.

Insurance
Look for periods of unusual claim frequency. Then do a fishbone diagram to understand underlying causes. This kind of issue usually has a large number of potential causes; the fishbone diagram enables screening to the critical few.

INSTRUCTIONS FOR FISHBONE DIAGRAMS

In these diagrams, the specific problem of interest is normally the "head" of the fish. Then there are six "bones" on which we list input variables that affect the problem head.

Each bone has a category of input variables that should be listed. Separating the input variables into six different categories, each with its own characteristics, triggers us to make sure that no input variable is missed. The six categories are Measurements, Materials, Men, Methods, Machines, and Environment. (Some people remember these as "five M's and one E.") The six categories are what make the fishbone diagram more effective than a single-column list of all the input variables.

Ideally, the input variables on a fishbone should come from a group of "experts" working together in one room. This enables a high degree of interaction between the experts. However, if meeting in one room is not feasible, it *is* possible to do this process on the telephone, using a computer to regularly send updated versions of the fishbone diagram to all the people contributing. It is important for all contributors to be able to see the fishbone diagram as it evolves because it will stimulate their thinking on the input variables. Figure 8–1 is an abbreviated example of a fishbone diagram drawn for a "roller groove error" problem.

After listing all the input variables, the same team of experts should pick the two or three key process input variables (KPIVs) they feel are most likely to be the culprits. Those are highlighted in boldface and capital letters on the fishbone diagram in Figure 8–1.

There are software packages that enable someone to fill in the blanks of standardized forms for the fishbone diagram. There are also free downloads on the Internet that provide forms that tie in with *Excel*. However, other than for the sake of neatness, doing them by hand does just as well. We don't want playing with computer software getting in the way of the primary goal of identifying the input variables.

FIGURE 8–1

Fishbone Diagram
Input Variables Affecting Roller Groove Error

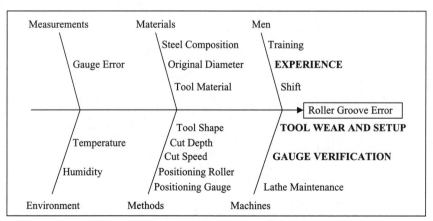

As you will see later in Chapter 13, the fishbone diagram is the recommended tool to identify what should be sampled in a process and to know what variables need to be kept in control during the sampling process. Without the kind of cause-and-effect analysis the fishbone diagram supports, the sampling will likely be less focused, take more time, and be fraught with error. This is because the amount of effort and control needed for good sampling and data collection is not trivial, so the amount of sampling must be minimized to allow everyone to get it right.

Sometimes just the process of doing the fishbone diagram leads to the solution because you are getting the experts together to discuss the problem, which would not have happened without a scheduled purpose.

Case Study: A Fishbone Diagram on Selling Art

The inputs for the Chapter 6 QFD case study, whose purpose was to identify how an artist friend could increase art sales, came from the fishbone diagram in Figure 8–2. That diagram was used to identify the key process input variables that in turn suggested the potential action items shown in the QFD.

FIGURE 8–2

Fishbone Diagram
Art Sales

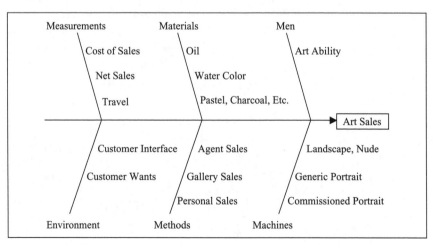

As you can see from the artwork case study, the usefulness of fishbone diagrams is not limited to industrial issues. Also, don't get too hung up on the specific names of the six categories. For example, listing "landscape, nude, generic portrait, and commissioned portrait" in the machines category may be a stretch for some of you. If it makes you feel better, change the name of the category. Just make sure that all the input variables get entered in one of the categories.

CHAPTER 8 REVIEW

1. The fishbone diagram is used primarily in the Define, Analyze, and Improve steps of the DMAIC process.
2. The purpose of a fishbone diagram is to have experts identify all the input variables that could be causing the problem of interest and to then look for a cause-and-effect relationship. Once we have a complete input variables list, we must attempt to identify the critical few key process input variables (KPIVs) to measure and further investigate.
3. The fishbone diagram is the preferred Six Sigma tool used to identify what should be sampled in a process and which variables need to be kept in control during the sampling process. Without the kind of cause-and-effect analysis the fishbone diagram supports, the required data sampling would be less focused.
4. Sometimes just the process of doing the fishbone diagram leads to the solution because you are getting the experts together to discuss the problem, which wouldn't happen without a scheduled purpose.
5. Use of the fishbone diagram is not limited to manufacturing. Virtually any problem can be tackled using this powerful tool.

CHAPTER 9

Simplified Process Flow Diagrams

What you will learn in this chapter is how to use a simplified process flow diagram to identify and examine all the possible causes for a problem. A process flow diagram can be used with a fishbone diagram, discussed in the previous chapter, to help identify the key process input variables (KPIVs).

It is important to know where and when input variables affect a process so you can see if that knowledge is consistent with where the problem is being seen. Of special interest are positions in the process where inspection or quality sorting takes place or where process data are collected. By looking at data from these positions, you may see evidence of a change or a problem. By noting where different operations take place, you can also see where issues can arise. Simplified process flow diagrams are used primarily in the Define, Analyze, and Improve steps of the DMAIC process.

A simplified process flow diagram works well when used in conjunction with a fishbone diagram. It can further screen the KPIVs that were already identified in the fishbone, minimizing where you will have to take additional samples or data.

There are software packages that enable users to fill in the blanks of standardized forms for a process flow diagram. There are

---

Simplified Process Flow Diagrams

Manufacturing
The simplified process flow diagram will focus an investigation by identifying where or when in the process KPIVs could be affecting the problem. Of special interest is where data are collected in the process.

Sales and Marketing
A simplified process flow diagram will assist you in identifying if the cause of low sales is regional, personnel, or some other factor. This information will allow you to focus on the likely area.

Accounting and Software Development
A simplified process flow diagram will help you pinpoint the specific problem areas in a system or program. This knowledge simplifies the debugging process. Software developers are very familiar with this process.

Receivables
A simplified process flow diagram will help you identify periods when delinquent receivables are higher than normal. This type of diagram may also help you design procedures, like giving discounts for early payment, to minimize the problem.

Insurance
A simplified process flow diagram may assist you in identifying an unusually high claims period versus a normal claims period.

---

also free downloads on the Internet that have forms that tie in with *Excel*. However, other than for the sake of neatness, doing them by hand works just as well.

INSTRUCTIONS FOR SIMPLIFIED PROCESS FLOW DIAGRAMS

A process flow diagram shows the relationships among the steps in a process or the components in a system, with arrows connecting all of the elements and showing the sequence of activities. Some texts and software for traditional process flow diagrams use additional geometrical shapes to differentiate between different process functions. I choose to keep it simple, only emphasizing where measurements or quality judgments are made. Figure 9–1 shows a simplified process flow diagram.

Just as with the fishbone diagram, the simplified process flow diagram is not limited to uses related to solving problems in a manufacturing process. Also, a simplified process flow diagram is not limited to being only a physical flow map. The flow could be related to time or process steps, not just place.

FIGURE 9–1

Simplified Process Flow Diagram
Roller Groove Machining

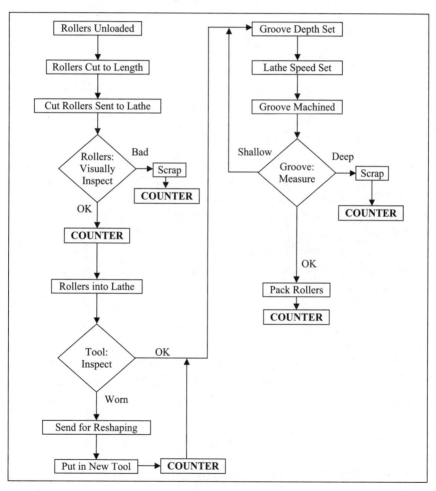

Figure 9–2 is a simplified process flow diagram on a non-manufacturing process. This process flow diagram is event based. It shows the steps someone would follow to get a book published.

Of course, in both of the above examples, the process flow diagrams are greatly simplified. In most of the areas in which you will use this tool, the situation will be very involved, with many decision points and many path options.

FIGURE 9–2

Simplified Process Flow Diagram
Book Publishing

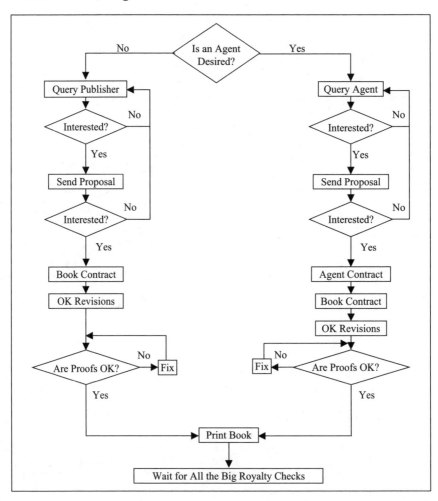

Case Study: A Rebuild of a Complex Piece of Production Equipment

This particular production machine was already the fastest of its kind in the world, and the plan was to speed it up an additional 8 percent. This would involve much design work and was going to cost over $1 million. There would be a three-week period during which the production plant would be down and the rebuild would take place. It was imperative that the machine be ready for production by the end of the three-week period. This was important because inventories would be low and within a few days after planned start-up, a shortage of the parts made on this machine would stop production of a more expensive assembly.

Since there were multiple teams responsible for different elements of this rebuild, including several outside contractors, a process flowchart was made for the total rebuild process, with every step shown. This process flowchart was developed in the months leading up to the rebuild of the machine, with everyone who was involved contributing and agreeing to the content and dates. This flowchart, which was time and element based, was delineated such that daily progress could be monitored. The total process flowchart took many sheets of chart paper and eventually covered 15 feet of a conference room wall.

In the middle of the rebuild, a visiting engineer saw the totally disassembled machine, with its parts all over the plant. The visiting engineer asked the project manager how he could possibly sleep nights. The project manager took the visitor into the conference room and showed him the process flowchart, where every contributing party was not only monitoring his or her own progress but also initialing and dating the flowchart steps as they were completed. The project manager explained that *this* was how he could sleep nights.

The project was completed on schedule with minimum hassle. Everyone involved was very pleased to have had the detailed process flowchart that had been completed before the heat of the battle.

Note that process flowcharts, as is true for most of the Six Sigma tools, are not new. They have been used in some format for many years. But since Six Sigma includes them as part of the Six Sigma arsenal, they are more likely to be considered and used than if they were thought of as a stand-alone option.

CHAPTER 9 REVIEW

1. Simplified process flow diagrams are used primarily in the Define, Analyze, and Improve steps of the DMAIC process.

2. A simplified process flow diagram will help pinpoint the area in which efforts should be concentrated. Of special interest in a process is where data are collected or quality

decisions are made since this information will often help focus the study on a defined process area.

3. Simplified process flow diagrams work well in conjunction with fishbone diagrams. By using the two, the areas to further investigate and sample are minimized.

4. The usefulness of a simplified process flow diagram is not limited to a physical flow map. The flow could be related to time or process steps, not just place.

5. Besides being used for problem solving, process flow diagrams can be used to configure a proposed new process.

CHAPTER 10

Visual Correlation Tests

What you will learn in this chapter is that visual correlation tests are another way to discover the key process input variables (KPIVs) that may have caused a change in a process or product. Visual correlation tests are straightforward and only require collecting data, making plots of that data, and then visually looking for correlations. Visual correlation tests are used primarily in the Define, Analyze, and Improve steps of the DMAIC process.

In some Six Sigma classes, regression analysis is used to find correlations. A mathematical curve is fit to a set of data, and techniques are used to measure how well the data fit these curves. The curves are then used to test for correlations.

Regression analysis requires some degree of skill, and it is generally not friendly to those who are not doing this kind of analysis almost daily. Thankfully, most Six Sigma work can be done using the tools already covered in this book, as long as someone is willing to do some visual examination of data and their related graphs.

Something has changed in a process or product, and we would like to discover the KPIVs that caused it. Time and position are our most valued friends in doing the analysis.

INSTRUCTIONS FOR CORRELATION TESTS

First isolate when and where the problem change took place. Do this by drawing a time plot or position plot of every measurement

---

Visual Correlation Tests

Manufacturing
Construct a time plot showing when a problem first appeared or when it comes and goes. Do similar time plots of the KPIVs to see if a change in any of these variables coincides with the timing of the problem change. If there are any such changes, do a controlled test to establish cause and effect for those KPIVs.

Sales and Marketing
For periods of unusually low sales activity, construct a time plot showing when the low sales started and stopped. Do similar time plots of the KPIVs to see if a change in any these variables coincides with the low sales periods. If they do, run a controlled test to establish cause and effect for that KPIV.

Accounting and Software Development
Construct a time plot of unusual accounting or computer issues. Do similar time plots of the KPIVs to see if a change in any these variables coincides with the issues. If they do, run a controlled test to establish cause and effect for that KPIV. The people in these areas usually respond well to this type of analysis.

Receivables and/or Insurance
Identify periods of higher-than-normal delinquent receivables or unusual claim frequency. Then construct a time plot of the problem and the related KPIVs. For any variable that shows coincident change, check for cause and/or effect with controlled tests.

---

of the process or product that is indicative of the change. These plots often define the time and/or position of the start of the change to a very narrow range. If the change indicated by the plot is large compared to other data changes before and after the incidence and the timing corresponds to the observed problem recognition, it is generally worthwhile to check for correlations.

The next thing to do is to look for correlations with input variables, using graphs of historical data. If the KPIVs are not already known, we must do a fishbone diagram or a process flow diagram to identify them. Do time plots or position plots of every KPIV, centering on the previously defined problem time period or position. Any input variable that changed at nearly the same time or position as the problem is suspect.

When there are multiple time and/or position agreements of change between the problem and an input variable, then do controlled tests where everything but the suspicious variable is kept constant. In this way cause-and-effect relationships can be established.

If more than one KPIV changed, there could be an interaction between these variables, but usually one KPIV will stand out. Looking at extended time periods will often rule out input variables that do not correlate consistently.

Numerical methods to test for statistically significant change will be covered later in the text. These tests can be used to identify significant change on the data just before the problem versus right after the problem begins. These tests can be used on both the problem data and the KPIV data. However, if there are a few or more instances of time agreement on change between the problem and the KPIV, these extra tests are often not needed. In any case, controlled tests will have to be run to prove a true cause-and-effect relationship between the suspect KPIV and the problem. If we cannot make the problem come and go by changing the suspect KPIV in a controlled manner, then we may not have not found the correct KPIV.

Figure 10–1 shows simplified plots of a problem and the process KPIVs (A, B, and C). This visual check is very easy and often obvious, once plots of the problem and the KPIVs are compared with each other.

KPIV B certainly looks suspicious, given that it had a change in the same time interval as the problem, matching both the beginning and the end of the time period. As a first test, expand the time of the data for both the process defect rate and the KPIV B to see if this change agreement is truly as unique and correlated as it appears in the Figure 10–1 limited data. If, in the expanded data, either the defect appeared without the change in the suspect KPIV or the KPIV changed without a related defect change, then the suspect KPIV is likely not correctly identified. Remember, however, that this test will never be definitive. It will only hint—albeit strongly—at the cause. A test set up to control all possible variables (except for KPIV B in Figure 10–1) will be required. We would intentionally change KPIV B as shown in the plot in Figure 10–1 and see if the problem responds similarly. Only then will we have truly established a cause-and-effect relationship.

FIGURE 10-1

Correlation Illustration Plots

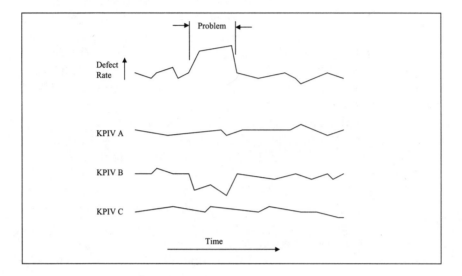

When time plots of variables are compared to the change we are studying, it is important that any inherent time shift be incorporated. For example, if a raw material is put into a storage bin with three days' previous inventory and if the material is used based on the timing of the material into the bin, this three-day

> **TIP**
> **Showing Cause and Effect**
>
> Correlation doesn't prove cause and effect. It just shows that two or more things happened to change at the same time or at the same position. There have been infamous correlations (stork sightings versus birth rates) that are just coincidental or have other explanations (people kept their houses warmer as the birth of a baby became imminent and the heat from the fireplaces attracted the storks).
>
> To show true cause and effect, you must run controlled tests where only the key test input variable is changed (just the births with no additional fireplace heat at the time of births) and its effect is measured (did the stork sightings still increase?). Normally, historical data can't be used to prove cause and effect because the data are too "noisy" and the other variables are not being controlled.

delay must be incorporated when looking for a correlation of that raw material to the process.

Case Study: Nonequivalent Aim

A manufacturing plant produced a projection lamp that used a metal reflector. When this lamp was inserted into the projector, it was critical that the projected light beam was aimed correctly, and there were quality criteria that specified what aim accuracy was required.

The lamp maker often had difficulty meeting these specifications; so they started a project to identify the contributors to this lamp-aim problem. One of the things they investigated was the contribution of the metal reflector.

The reflector manufacturer had as one of their quality checks their *own* aim check. They would put the reflector into a fixture, move a light source around until they got a uniform projected image, and then measure the degree to which the projected image was off a nominal target.

When the lamp maker reviewed these reflector aim readings, they found that the reflector manufacturer was regularly sending them reflectors with aim variations exceeding the aim allowance for the total lamp. The lamp maker felt satisfied that they had identified the root cause of their problem and proceeded to put tight specifications on the reflector aim readings.

Since the reflector manufacturer was having great difficulty meeting these new requirements, they asked for assistance from their home office engineering team.

One of the first things this engineering team did was construct plots of the lamp aim versus the reflector aim. They saw no visual correlation! Someone then noticed that the manner of determining *aim* was dramatically different for the reflector than it was for the lamp. When determining lamp aim, the light source was put in a nominal mechanical position versus the reflector. When aim was determined in the reflector operation, the light source was first moved to optimize the projected image, *then* the aim was read.

The engineer then ran a test in which the reflector aim was read with the light source kept in the mechanical nominal position. When these aim readings were plotted versus the resultant lamp aim, there *was* a strong visual correlation.

The method for reading reflector aim was then changed, and new specifications were developed using this new aim method. The reflector manufacturer was now able to make the product acceptable to their lamp customer, and the lamp aim problem vanished.

The tool that triggered the realization that reflector aim (as it was originally measured) was not the culprit causing bad lamp aim was the visual check for correlations on the plotted data of reflector aim versus the lamp aim. No visual correlation was seen. Equally, there *was* a visual correlation between reflector aim and lamp aim when they were both read with the light source in the mechanical nominal position.

These initial observations were followed up with quantitative statistical tests that checked for significant change, but the correlation tests done on visual plots were the breakthrough trigger. And, of course, controlled tests were needed to prove cause and effect.

CHAPTER 10 REVIEW

1. Correlation tests are used primarily in the Define, Analyze, and Improve steps of the DMAIC process.

2. In some Six Sigma classes, regression analysis is used to find correlations. These methods require a high degree of skill, and they generally are not friendly to those who are not doing this kind of analysis almost daily.

3. Something has changed in a process or product, and the goal is to discover the key process input variable (KPIV) that caused it. Time and position are the critical factors in performing the analysis. Using data plots first isolates when and where the problem change is taking place.

4. Look for a matching time period or position change on data plots of all input variables. Identify all KPIVs that have a change that correlates with the problem.

5. Test for a cause-and-effect relationship by running controlled tests with only the suspect KPIV being changed.

6. Statistical tests for significance, which will be covered later in the text, can also assist in checking for correlations. But often the visual correlation using data plots is sufficient, especially when there are multiple correlations of timing between the problem and a KPIV.

CHAPTER 11

Reality-Based Tolerances

What you will learn in this chapter is that most tolerances have *not* been determined by application needs. Tolerances often have little to do with what is really required. In fact, one general manager at GE maintained that "spec" was often short for "speculation" rather than for specification! Tolerances can and should be questioned. Tolerances apply to the Improve and Control steps in the DMAIC process.

Some Six Sigma books treat tolerances as part of "Design for Six Sigma," which is a somewhat more technical aspect of Six Sigma. However, the issues on tolerances discussed in this chapter are *not* technical in that they involve just plain erroneous tolerances. These tolerances may be causing problems or losses to either the supplier or customer. Solving these issues will often drive huge savings with no other effort.

Correct tolerances are important to both the supplier, who has to adjust his or her process to supply a product within the documented tolerances, and the customer who is getting a product presumably within the advertised tolerances.

INSTRUCTIONS FOR DETERMINING REALITY-BASED TOLERANCES

Determining correct tolerances does not normally require anything more technical than running tests on various levels of imperfect parts to determine what the customer really needs.

The initial tolerance on a part is often based on what machine the designer believes will make the part. The tightest tolerance the machine can achieve is then used. Note that it is the *tightest* tolerance that is often picked, not the average tolerance. Or the designer just copies the tolerance from a previously supplied part that looks similar. An analysis of the customer's real need is seldom done.

Sometime later the customer may have some issue with the part and complain. Then the tolerance is tightened—whether or not the issue involved the tolerance. Because many tolerances have evolved in this haphazard manner, there is a large savings potential in determining what is really required in a tolerance.

Case Study: Required Tolerances on Forming Pins

Pins having a complex shape were being used to form a stepped impression in a formed product. The depth of this impression was critical to assembly operations using this product, and the customer had periodically complained that the variations of the impression were excessive. So, in response, the tolerance on this pin had been reduced several times, making the pin very expensive.

When an engineer pulled out historical data on the impression depths, he saw little improvement despite this tightening of pin tolerances. He then started to analyze the problem with more care. He discovered that the mold in which the pin was seated had a very loose tolerance on the related pin seating surface. Apparently everyone assumed that this mold seating surface was tightly controlled, so they went after the pin variation only.

It added no cost to put a reasonable tolerance on this mold seating plane. Once this dimension was under control, tests were run to determine what tolerance was required on the pins. The results based on real need allowed the pin tolerance to be doubled. This allowed the producer of the formed part to meet specifications on the stepped-impression depth, while saving on pin costs.

Although we normally think of tolerances as being related to industrial parts, many other things have tolerances. A passing/failing grade in a school subject is a tolerance that may or may not reflect what is truly required to know the subject satisfactorily. Performance criteria for employees may be too loose or too tight, or they may not even measure the right thing. Safety requirements and pollution regulations may not be scientifically based, but instead they may have been established due to political pressures or based on past published criteria.

TIP

Reviewing Tolerances on Real Parts and/or Processes

On any part that is difficult or expensive to make because of tight tolerances, review the tolerances based on real application requirements. You should question any limitations or measures of acceptance placed on anything that is causing issues.

Before we work on any problem, we should spend some time in trying to ascertain whether the requirements (tolerances) are correct and based on real need.

CHAPTER 11 REVIEW

1. Tolerances apply to the Improve and Control steps in the DMAIC process.

2. Tolerances are seldom calculated based on requirements, so there are potential savings to be realized by reviewing tolerances that cause issues.

3. When there is a problem with a part, sometimes the reaction is to tighten tolerances on that part, whether or not the tolerance is the issue. This often makes the tolerance tighter than needed or makes the tolerance meaningless.

Getting Good Data

Conditio sine qua non   (Necessary condition)

—Latin saying

Part Three, which includes Chapters 12 through 14, is concerned with data type, collecting samples, and verifying that gauges give good measurements.

Data are either variables data or proportional data. Chapter 12 gives guidelines for determining which kind of data you have.

We have to collect random and valid samples. This process is not without challenges, as discussed in Chapter 13. This chapter also discusses why both average and variation of data are important and why they are often analyzed separately.

Any gauge that is measuring variables data must be checked to make sure that the errors generated by the gauge itself aren't so large that they make the measurements worthless. Chapter 14 addresses this issue.

CHAPTER 12

Types of Data

What you will learn in this chapter is that all the statistics that we use in Six Sigma draw on only two types of data: variables and proportional. We will show how to determine which type of data you have and discuss the advantages of each. Specific examples will be shown to minimize any confusion. This chapter also discusses data discrimination, which is used to determine whether the steps in numerical data are small enough such that the data can be used as variables.

VARIABLES DATA

Variables data are normally related to measurements expressed as decimals. This type of data can theoretically be measured to whatever degree of accuracy desired, the only limitations being the measuring device and the decimal places to which you collect the data. This is why variables data are sometimes called *continuous data*.

PROPORTIONAL DATA

Proportional data are always ratios or probabilities. Proportional data are often expressed as decimals, but these decimals are the ratios of two numbers rather than being physical measurements. Proportional data are either ratios of attributes (good/bad, good/total, yes/no, and so on), or ratios of discrete or stepped numerical values.

You will see in the following chapters that, for statistical analysis, variables data are preferred over proportional data because variables data allow us to make decisions on fewer samples.

DATA DISCRIMINATION

Most Six Sigma texts ignore the fact that some data need interpretation to determine if they can be analyzed as variables. The following example shows how this determination can be made.

The following list consists of individual ages collected from a group of people aged 50 to 55. Assume that the data are going to be used in a study of the incidence of diseases:

Ages

53.2	55.0	53.4
54.1	52.7	52.3
50.2	54.5	53.4
54.3	54.8	Etc.
51.3	54.2	

Since the data were collected in units equal to tenths of a year, there is good discrimination of the data versus the five-year study period. Good discrimination means that the data steps are small compared to the five-year range being studied. These data have measurement steps of tenths of a year because the data were collected and displayed to one-decimal-point resolution. Theoretically the data could have been measured and displayed with three decimal points of resolution by using the actual days of birth or to an even a higher degree of accuracy if birth times on the days of birth were known.

Rule of Thumb on Variables Data Discrimination

On variables data the measurement resolution should be sufficient to give at least 10 steps within the range of interest.

For example, if data are collected on a part with a 0.050-inch tolerance, the data measurement steps should be no larger than 0.005 inch to be able to analyze that data as variables.

In the prior data example on ages, since the data are displayed to the first decimal point, there are 50 discrimination steps in the five-year study period (5.0 divided by 0.1), which is greater than the 10-step minimum rule of thumb.

Let's suppose that the above age data had been collected as follows:

Ages

53	55	53
54	53	52
50	55	53
54	55	Etc.
51	54	

The data now have to be analyzed as proportions because of the decision to collect the data as discrete whole numbers. With these broad steps there are only five discrete steps within the five-year study period (5 divided by 1), which is below the 10-discrimination-step minimum for variables data. To analyze these data as proportions, for example, we could study the proportion of people 52 years of age or younger or the proportion of people 53 years of age.

The original age data could also have been collected as attributes, where each person from the above group of people was asked if he or she was 53 or older. The collected data would then have looked like the following:

Is Your Age 53 or Older?

Yes	Yes	Yes
Yes	No	No
No	Yes	Yes
Yes	Yes	Etc.
No	Yes	

These are *attribute data*, which can be studied only as proportional data. For example, the proportion of yes or no answers could be calculated directly from the data, and then the resultant proportion could be used in an analysis.

What we saw in the above examples is that data collected on an event can often be either variables or proportional, based on the manner they are collected and their resolution or discrimination. Attribute data, however, are always treated as a proportion (after determining a ratio).

There are some data that are numerical but only available at discrete levels. Shoe size is an example. By definition the steps are discrete, with no information available for values between the shoe sizes. Discrete data are often treated as proportions because the steps usually limit the discrimination versus the range of interest.

Let's look at another example, this time using shaft dimensions. Assume that a shaft has a maximum allowable diameter of 1.020 inches and a minimum allowable diameter of 0.080 inch, which is a tolerance of 0.040 inch. Here is the first set of data:

Shaft Diameter, Inches

1.008	1.000	1.009
0.982	1.009	1.014
0.996	1.002	Etc.
1.017	1.003	
0.997	0.991	

Since the dimensions are to the third decimal place, these measurement steps are small compared to the need (the 0.040-inch tolerance). Since there are 40 discrimination steps (0.040 inch divided by 0.001 inch), these data can be analyzed as variables data.

Suppose, however, that the same shafts were measured as follows:

Shaft Diameter, Inches

1.01	1.00	1.01
0.98	1.01	1.01
1.00	1.00	Etc.
1.02	1.00	
1.00	0.99	

Since the accuracy of the numbers is now only to two decimal places, the steps within the 0.040-inch tolerance are only four

(0.040 inch divided by 0.010 inch), which is below the rule-of-thumb 10-discrimination-step minimum. We must therefore analyze these data as proportions. For example, we could calculate the proportion of shafts that are below 1.00 inch and use that information in an analysis.

Similarly, the same data could have been collected as attributes, checking whether the shafts were below 1.000 inch in diameter, yes or no, determined by a go/no-go gauge set at 1.000 inch. The collected data would then look like the list below:

Is the Shaft below 1.000 inch in Diameter?

No	No	No
Yes	No	No
Yes	No	Etc.
No	No	
Yes	Yes	

These are attribute data, which can be analyzed only as proportional data. The proportion of yes or no answers can be calculated and then used in an analysis.

Again, what we saw in the above example is that data collected on the same event could be either variables or proportional, based on the manner they were measured and the discrimination.

This concept is fairly straightforward. Since all measurements at some point become stepped due to measurement limitations, these steps must be reasonably small compared to the range of interest if we wish to use the data as variables.

Any data that do not qualify as variables must be treated as proportions. The proportions could be something like the ratio of red and green candies in a box of candies of various colors. It could be the proportions of bad parts in shipments. It could be the percentages of people that are over 65 years of age. In all of these cases, however, the required sample sizes for analysis will be much greater than they would be if we had variables data.

Let's look at one more example. A manufacturer of boat sails wants to analyze his material costs versus quality losses when the material for a sail is cut with various amounts of excess material. He measures many material samples with a yardstick with ¼-inch increments, and his measurements go from 10 inches of extra material to 25 inches of extra material. His measurements are in steps of ¼ inch. Can he analyze these data as variables, even though they are obviously stepped? Let's look at the discrimination. Since the dimensions range from 10 to 25 inches and the steps are ¼ inch, there are a total of $15 \times 4 = 60$ steps, which is far more than the 10 minimum. So, although these dimensions were collected in fractions with a yardstick, by converting the measurements to decimals, they can be analyzed as variables data.

CHAPTER 12 REVIEW

1. All the statistics that we use in Six Sigma are one of only two types of data: variables and proportional.

2. Variables data are normally measurements expressed as decimals. These data can theoretically be measured to whatever degree of accuracy desired, which is why they are sometimes called *continuous data.*

3. A rule of thumb is that on variables data the measurement resolution should be sufficient to give at least 10 steps within the range of interest.

4. Proportional data are always ratios or probabilities. Proportional data are often expressed as decimals, but these decimals are ratios rather than physical measurements. Proportional data are either ratios of attributes (good/bad, good/total number, yes/no, and so on), or ratios of discrete or stepped numerical values.

5. Any data that do not qualify as variables must be treated as proportions.

CHAPTER 13

Collecting Samples

What you will learn in this chapter is how to take good samples and get good data. This chapter also discusses why both averages and variation of data are important and why we do analysis separately on both.

In later chapters you will see how to calculate minimum sample sizes and how to verify that a gauge is giving data that are sufficient for your needs. Just as important, however, is making sure that your sample and data truly represent the population of the process you wish to measure. The whole intent of sampling is to be able to analyze a process or population and get valid results without measuring every part, so sampling details are extremely important.

We have all seen the problems pollsters have in predicting election outcomes based on sampling. In general the problem has *not* been in the statistical analysis of the data or in the sample size. The problem has been picking a group of people to sample that truly represents the electorate!

The population is not uniform. There are pockets of elderly, wealthy, poor, Democrats, Republicans, urbanites, and suburbanites, each with their own agendas that may affect the way they vote. And neither the pockets nor their agendas are uniform or static. So, even using indicators from past elections does not guarantee that a pollster's sample will replicate the population as a whole.

Issues in Getting Good Data

Manufacturing
Samples and the resultant data have to represent the total population, yet processes controlling the population are often changing dramatically due to people, environment, equipment, and similar factors.

Sales
Sales forecasts often use sampling techniques in their predictions. Yet the total market may have many diverse groups to sample affected by many external drivers, like the economy.

Marketing
What data should be used to judge a marketing campaign's effectiveness, since so many other factors are changing at the same time?

Software Development
What are the main causes of software crashes, and how would you get data to measure the "crash resistance" of competing software?

Receivables
How would you get good data on the effectiveness of a program intended to reduce overdue receivables, when factors like the economy exert a strong influence and change frequently?

Insurance
How can data measuring customer satisfaction with different insurance programs be compared when the people covered by the programs are not identical?

The problem of sampling and getting good data has several key components. First, the people and the methods used for taking the samples and data affect the randomness and accuracy of both. Second, the population is diverse and often changing, sometimes quite radically. These changes occur over time and can be affected by location. To truly reflect a population, anyone sampling and using data must be aware of all these variables and somehow get valid data despite them.

HAWTHORNE EFFECT

As soon as anyone goes out to measure a process, things change. Everyone pays more attention. The process operators are more likely to monitor their process and quality inspectors are likely to be more effective in segregating defects. The resultant product you are sampling is not likely to represent that of a random process. This is even true when people are polled on an issue, in that their answers for polling purposes may be the result of far more careful thought than their answers would be under other circumstances.

There have been many studies done on how people react to having someone pay attention to them. Perhaps the most famous is the Hawthorne study, which was done at a large Bell Western manufacturing facility—the Hawthorne Works—in Cicero, Illinois, from 1927 to 1932. This study showed that any gain realized during a controlled test often came from the positive interaction between the people conducting the test and the participants, and also from the interaction between the participants. The people may begin to work together as a team to get positive results. The actual variable change being tested was often not the driver of any improvement.

One of the tests at the Hawthorne facility involved measuring how increasing the light level would influence productivity. The productivity did indeed increase where the light level was increased. But in a control group where the light level was *not* changed, productivity also improved by the same amount. It was apparently the attention given to both groups by the researchers that was the positive influence, not the light level. In fact, when the light level was restored to its original level, the productivity remained improved for some time. Thus this effect of attention on research subjects has become known as the *Hawthorne effect*.

Any research data that show an improvement must be suspect due to the Hawthorne effect. Your best protection from making an incorrect assumption about improvement is to take data simultaneously from a parallel line with an identical process (control group) but without the change. However, the people in both groups should have had the same attention, attended the same meetings, and so on. An alternative method is to collect line samples just before and just after the change is implemented, but do so after all the meetings and other interactions have concluded. The before samples would be compared to the after samples, with the assumption that any Hawthorne effect would be included in both.

There was a different result, however, in another study in the same Hawthorne facility. In this case, the participants of the study were afraid that the test results were going to negatively affect their jobs, and so, as a group, they had agreed before the study began that their productivity would *not* improve, and of course it didn't. Running a test in this environment would make it very difficult to ascertain whether a change was good or bad. In this kind of environment, the only way to get good data is to do a surreptitious change unless the change is so basic to the process that its results can't be denied.

OTHER SAMPLING DIFFICULTIES

If you ask an inspector to pick up and inspect a product at random, there is a chance that the sample the inspector chooses will be biased toward any product with a visible defect. This is because inspectors are accustomed to looking for defects and because they believe you are there because of problems with defects, so they want to be helpful.

I once ran a test where product was being inspected online, paced by the conveyor speed. I collected the rejected product and isolated the packed "good" product from this same time period. Without telling the inspectors, I then mixed the defective product with the good packed product and had the same inspectors inspect this remixed product offline, where the inspectors weren't machine paced. The defect rate almost doubled. Of further interest was that the customer had not been complaining about the quality of the product inspected online.

When the product was inspected without time restraints, the quality criteria apparently tightened, even though no one had changed the criteria. Or maybe the inspectors had just become more effective. Another possibility is that the inspectors felt that I was checking on their effectiveness in finding all the defects, so they were being extra conservative in interpreting the criteria. In any case, someone using data from the offline inspection would get a defect rate almost double that seen online. Therefore, if someone had implemented a change and was checking its effectiveness by checking for defects offline, the change would have had to reduce the actual defects in half for the data to even look equivalent to the historical data from online inspection. Obviously this would be problematic.

Time considerations are not the only influence on quality criteria, as I saw in another situation. To check the optics on a parabolic reflector, an inspector would insert the reflector into a fixture that seated the reflector precisely over a light source. The inspector would then make a judgment on the quality of the resultant projected image. Too many "poor" readings would cause the product to be scrapped and the reflector-forming process to be reset.

As a test, on a day with an unusually high incidence of good optical readings, I collected the relatively few reflectors that had poor readings. On a later date, when the process was generating a lot of poor optical readings, I reintroduced the reflectors that had earlier been judged poor. They were now judged as good. Because of the qualitative nature of the criteria, the judgment of good or poor apparently became relative to the average optics that the inspector was seeing.

Sometimes people become very defensive (or maybe even offensive) when samples are taken from their process. In one of the case studies I relate later, the employees of a manufacturing plant thought that their defects were caused by bad raw materials. When a team began collecting defects on one of the plant's production lines and correlating them back to specific problems on that line, the line operator grieved to his union that he was being harassed because the engineering team was not looking at the raw materials, which the operator was *sure* were causing the problem. Incidentally, the problems did prove to be related to the line and were not caused by raw materials.

Case Study: Cheating the System

A manufacturing plant had six production lines. A quality technician would take a 5-minute sample every hour from each line. The technician would rotate through the plant in a regular pattern, so every hour a sample was taken at a predictable time on each line. Based on this sample, the prior hour's production was either released or held for additional quality checks.

The quality sample was taken at a position 15 minutes downstream from where the product was produced, after a heat treatment process. One of the experienced operators was aware of these quality checks and did not like his product being held for quality issues. So he got into the habit of going to the conveyor leading to the heat treatment process 15 minutes before his line's quality check, and for 5 minutes he would remove from the conveyor any questionable product, putting it back on the conveyor after the 5 minutes had expired. In this way his product always passed the quality test. He was giving the inspector a biased sample.

No one knew that this was going on. No one was tracking the customer complaints based on production line, and no one noticed that this operator's product was always released by the quality check. Finally, someone saw the operator doing his preinspection.

The quality manager then changed the sampling procedure such that the quality technician used a random number generator to determine which line to sample next. That solved the problem.

Case Study: Adjusting Data

I was watching a person inspecting product on a high-speed production line. On a regular basis, she would pick up a random product from the conveyor and place it onto a fixture having several electronic gauges that took key measurements. These measurements were displayed on the inspector's computer screen and then automatically sent to the quality database unless the inspector overrode the sending of the data. The inspector was supposed to use the override only if she saw a very specific problem such as the product's not being seated properly in the fixture, necessitating a new reading on that product.

As I was observing, I saw the inspector periodically override the sending of the data even though I saw no apparent problem with the seating. When I asked the inspector why she was not sending the data, she replied that the readings looked unusual and she didn't think they were representative of the majority of product being measured. She didn't want what she thought was erroneous data sent to the system, so she overrode the sending of the data and went to the next product. She didn't even reread the product.

She proudly told me that she had been doing that for years and that she had trained other inspectors accordingly. So much for using *those* data! Anyone running a test on this line and then taking his or her own quality samples would likely find more variation in the self-inspected samples than the quality system's historical data would show.

Getting random samples from a conveyor belt is not always easy. Production equipment can have multiple heads that load onto a conveyor belt in a nonrandom fashion. Some of the heads on the production machine may have all of their products sent down one side of the conveyor. The result is that someone taking samples from one side of the conveyor belt will never see product from some of the production heads.

The start-up of any piece of equipment often generates an unusually high incidence of defects. After a shift change, it may take some time for the new operator to get a machine running to his or her own parameters, during which time the quality may suffer. Absenteeism and vacations cause inexperienced people to operate equipment, which in turn generally causes lower quality. Maintenance schedules can often be sensed in product quality. Another influence on quality is scheduling—which production line is scheduled on which product. And, of course, there are variables of humidity, temperature, and so on.

Overall quality is a composite of all the above variables and more. In fact, a case could be made that many quality issues come from these "exception" mini-populations. So how can you possibly sample such that all these variables are taken into account?

First, you probably can't take samples in all the possible combinations listed above. In fact, before you begin to take any samples, you have to go back to the DMAIC process and define the problem. Only with a good definition of the problem will you be able to ascertain what to sample.

UNDERSTANDING HOW DATA WILL BE USED

Before we begin to sample data, we have to understand how we are going to use that data. In Six Sigma we generally are interested in how the average of the data differs from a nominal target and in the variation between the data. What follows is some discussion on how we describe data in Six Sigma terms and why we collect data in the manner we do.

Sigma

One of the ways to describe the measure of the variation of a product is to use the mathematical term *sigma*. We will learn more about sigma and how to calculate this value as we proceed, but for now it is enough to know that the smaller the sigma value, the smaller the amount of process variation; the larger the sigma value, the greater the amount of process variation. In general, you want to minimize sigma (variation). Since the sigma calculation is normally done on a computer or calculator, it is more important that you gain a sense that sigma is a measure of the data spread (variation) than it is to be too involved with the detailed calculation of sigma.

Ideally the sigma value is small in comparison to the allowable tolerance on a part or process. If so, the process variation will be small compared with the tolerance a customer requires. When this is the case, the process is "tight" enough that, even if the process is somewhat off center, the process produces product well within the customer's needs.

Many companies have processes with a relatively large variation compared to their customers' needs (a relatively high sigma value compared to the allowable tolerance). These companies run at an average ±3 sigma level (a 3 sigma process). This means that 6 sigma (±3 sigma) fit between the tolerance limits. The smaller the sigma, the more sigma that fit within the tolerance, as you can see in Figure 13–1.

Sigma level is calculated by dividing the process's allowable tolerance (upper specification minus lower specification) by twice the process's sigma value because the sigma level of a process is stated as a plus-or-minus value.

FIGURE 13–1

Two Different Process Sigmas

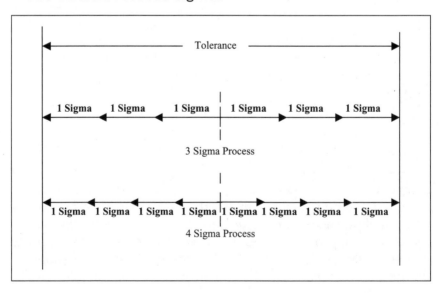

DEFINITION

$$\text{Process sigma level} = \pm \frac{\text{process tolerance}}{2 \times \text{process sigma value}}$$

As an example, suppose a bearing grinding process has the following measurements:

Sigma = 0.002 inch

Maximum allowable bearing diameter = 1.006 inches

Minimum allowable bearing diameter = 0.994 inch

So the tolerance is 1.006 − 0.994 = 0.012 inch. Putting these values into the process-sigma-level formula:

$$\text{Process sigma level} = \pm \frac{\text{process tolerance}}{2 \times \text{process sigma value}}$$

$$= \pm \frac{0.012 \text{ inch}}{2 \times 0.002 \text{ inch}}$$

$$= \pm 3$$

So this process is running at ±3 sigma, or, in the terms of Six Sigma, this is a 3 sigma process.

As you will see later in the book, a 3 sigma process generates 99.73 percent good product, or 997,300 good parts for every 1,000,000 parts produced. This means that there are 2,700 defective products for every 1,000,000 parts produced (or 2,700 input errors per 1,000,000 computer entries, and so on).

Note that some statistics books show the defect level for a 3 sigma process as a radically higher number. If you see a defect level of 66,807 defects per million for a 3 sigma process (versus the 2,700 indicated above), it is because the other book is using Motorola's Six Sigma defect table that includes an assumed 1.5 sigma long-term process drift. The 2,700 defects per million used in this book is consistent with the statistics tables that you will cover in Chapter 16. In any case, just don't be surprised if some books include the 1.5 sigma drift in their numbers. Including or not including this long-term assumed drift is largely academic as long as you are consistent in your data comparisons. Since almost all Six Sigma work you will be doing involves data collected and compared over a relatively short period of time (several days or weeks), including an assumed long-term drift will just confuse any analysis and give misleading results. Chapter 20 of this book will address how to minimize any long-term process drift.

The defects associated with a 3 sigma process are costly, causing scrap, rework, returns, and lost customers. Eliminating this lost product has the potential to be a profitable "hidden factory" because all the costs and efforts have been expended to produce the product, but it's unusable.

The potential efficiency and quality gains of implementing Six Sigma make it a viable alternative to sending manufacturing offshore. There are companies in this country that are so efficient that overseas companies, even with their lower labor costs, cannot compete. The Six Sigma process helps companies reach that competitive goal by reducing losses.

Just for interest, a Six Sigma process runs with a variation such that ±6 sigma, including the Motorola assumed process drift, or 12 sigma, fit within the tolerance limits. This will generate 3 defects per million parts produced. This was the original quality goal of this methodology, and it is how the name "Six Sigma" became associated with this methodology. This extremely low defect incidence is not required in most real-world situations, and the cost of getting to that quality level is usually not justified. However, getting the quality to a level that the customer is extremely happy and supplier losses are very low is generally a cost-effective goal.

Average and Variation

It is important to differentiate between the error caused by the average measurement being different from a nominal target and the error caused by variations in measurements within the product or process.

No one knows how to make anything perfect. For example, if you were to buy fifty 1.000-inch-diameter bearings and then measure the bearings, you would find that they are not exactly 1.000 inch in diameter. They may be extremely close to 1.000 inch, but if you measure them carefully, you will find that the bearings are not exactly 1.000 inch.

The bearings will vary from the 1.000-inch nominal diameter in two different ways. First, the *average* diameter will not be exactly 1.000 inch. The average deviation from the target 1.000 inch is due to the bearing manufacturing process being off center.

The second reason that the bearings will differ from the target is that there will be some spread of measurements around the average bearing diameter. This spread of dimensions may be extremely small, but there will be a spread. This is due to the bearing process *variation*.

If the combination of the off-center bearing process and the bearing process variation is *small* compared to your needs (tolerance), then you will be satisfied with the bearings. If the combination of the off-center bearing process and the bearing process variation is *large* compared to your needs, then you will *not* be satisfied with the bearings. The Six Sigma methodology strives to make the combined effect of an off-center process and process variation small compared to the need (tolerance).

Let's suppose that the bearings you purchased were all larger in diameter than the 1.000-inch nominal diameter. Figure 13–2 illustrates the diameters of these bearings, including the variation. Since the maximum diameter as illustrated is less than the maximum tolerance, these bearings would be acceptable.

FIGURE 13–2

Bearing Diameters

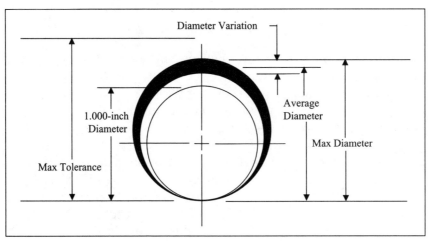

FIGURE 13–3

Off-Center Process and Process Variation

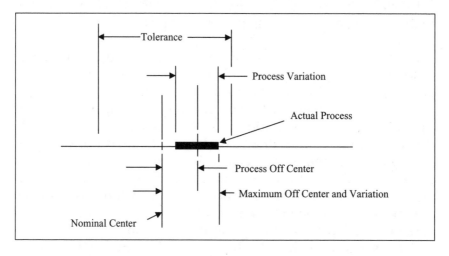

Figure 13–3 shows another way to look at the combination of an off-center process and process variation. This is an important concept to grasp because when you do Six Sigma projects, you have to worry about both issues: off center and variation. The combination is what affects total quality, but we often analyze them separately because the causes and solutions for each may be different.

Off-Center Processes

You have a dimensional problem on some ground pins. Is the problem that the grinding process is off center and initial data indicate that on the average they run too large? Or do you have a problem that all order takers are consistently making too many errors on order quantities? Or are almost all orders on a product being filled late? If a problem is of this nature, it is best addressed by improving the whole process, not focusing on the variation caused by the exception mini-populations. If being off center is the issue, then collecting samples and/or data and measuring change are a lot easier than they would be if you had to gather samples and/or data on each peculiar part of the population.

When attempting to measure your success on centering a process or changing the process average, you want to collect samples or use data that represent a "normal" process, both before and after any process adjustment. You don't want samples from any of the temporary mini-populations.

One of the ways to identify the normal population is to make a fishbone diagram where the head of the fish is "nonnormal populations." In this way the bones of the fish (the variables) will be all the variables that cause a population to be other than normal. You will then make sure that the time period in which you collect samples and/or data does not have any of the conditions listed on the fishbone.

Let's look at an example. Let's say the problem is the aforementioned issue that ground pins are generally running too large. Let's look at the fishbone diagram for this problem in Figure 13–4.

We can use the key process input variables (KPIVs) shown on this fishbone to determine which one(s) would likely cause the ground pin diameters to run off center, generally too large. The expert-picked KPIVs are experience of the operator, grinder wheel wear and setup, and gauge verification.

FIGURE 13–4

Fishbone Diagram
Input Variables Affecting Pin Diameter Errors

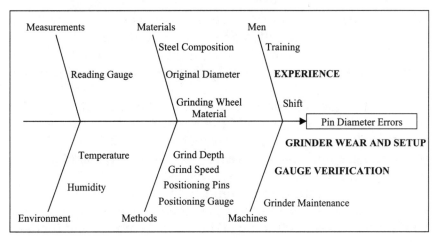

The experience of the operator would perhaps cause this issue for short periods but not for long periods as an ongoing problem. At times we would expect to have an experienced operator. Gauge setup and verification could account for the problem since the gauge could be reading off center such that the diameters would be generally too large. However, for this example, let's assume we check and are satisfied that the simplified gauge verifications (which will be covered in detail in the next chapter) have been done on schedule and correctly.

That leaves grinding wheel wear and setup. Grinding wheel wear could cause the diameters to change, but then the cycle would start over as the grinding wheel is changed. However, if the *grinding wheel setup* is incorrect, it could position the grinding wheel incorrectly all the time. This could conceivably cause the diameters to be generally high. So this is the variable we want to test.

We will want to test having the operator set the grinding wheel up with a different nominal setting to see if this will make the process more on center. We want to conduct random sampling during the process with the grinding wheel setup being the only variable that we change.

Since the effect of grinding wheel setup is what we want to measure, we want to control all the other input variables. As in the fishbone diagram in Figure 13–4, we especially want experienced people working on the process and want to be sure that the simplified gauge verification was done. These were the input variables that had been defined by the experts as being critical. We will also use a grinding wheel with average wear so that grinding wheel wear is not an issue. The test length for getting samples will be short enough that any additional grinding wheel wear during the test will be negligible.

We will use an experienced crew on the day shift, verifying that the pin material is correct and the grinder is set up correctly (grind depth, grind speed, and position of pin and gauge). We will make sure grinder maintenance has been done and that the person doing the measurements is experienced. We will minimize the effects of temperature and humidity by taking samples and/or data on the normal process and then immediately performing the test with the revised setup and taking the test samples and/or data.

TIP

Getting Good Samples and Data

Use good problem definition, a fishbone diagram, and any of the other qualitative tools to minimize the number of variables you have to test and then do a good job controlling the other variables during the test.

We will take samples and/or data only during these control periods.

Note that we used the fishbone to both show the KPIVs and to help pick the input variables we logically concluded could be causing the issue. Without this process of elimination, we would have had to test many more times. By limiting and controlling our tests, we can concentrate on getting the other variables under control, at least as much as possible.

If this test on grinding wheel setup did not solve the problem of pin diameters being too large, we would then go back and review our logic, perhaps picking another variable to test.

Sample sizes and needed statistical analysis will be covered in later chapters. In this chapter we are emphasizing only the non-numerical problems related to getting good data.

The example I just gave pertained to manufacturing. But what if the problem is in an office, like the earlier-mentioned issue of almost all order takers' making too many errors related to order quantity? Again, we would use a trusty fishbone diagram, as in Figure 13–5, with the head being order-quantity errors. Let's assume that this is the fishbone completed by a group of experts. These experts could have included experienced order takers, their managers, employees who pack the orders, billing staff, customer service personnel, and the customers.

The KPIVs picked by the experts are order rate, experience, and input form. Let's see which of these KPIVs make sense as being the cause of the problem as defined.

The order rate would vary, with some time periods having a low order rate. This isn't consistent with our problem definition that the order-quantity error incidence is too high consistently, so order rate is not the variable that we will test initially. Experience presumably varies among the order takers, so again that is not consistent with the problem definition that almost all the order

FIGURE 13–5

Fishbone Diagram
Input Variables Affecting Order-Quantity Errors

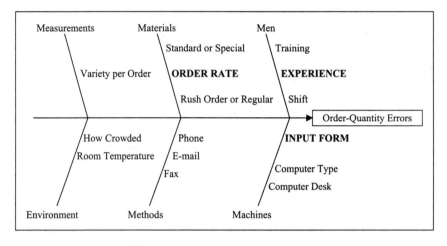

takers were making too many errors on order quantities. Only the input form looks as if it would affect most order takers consistently.

So we want to test if a redesign of the form that the order takers use can minimize the errors on order quantities. Just as we did in the manufacturing example, we will want to control all the variables except the one we wish to test and to collect our samples and/or data only during these controlled periods. Of special concern to control are the KPIVs shown in capital letters because these are the variables the experts identified as most likely to affect order-quantity errors.

So we will review only orders taken by experienced order takers during periods of time that the input of orders is at a somewhat average rate (that is, not exceptionally high or low). We will do this on the day shift, making sure that the room temperature and people density in the room where orders are taken are pretty much normal. To take out the effect of the different ordering methods, we will evaluate only orders taken by phone. The base sample data to get the normal order-quantity error rate will be taken on one day; the test samples with the new form will be done the following day.

Centering or Variation?

The above examples showed ways to get good samples and/or data when the problem definition indicated that the problem was related to a process not centered, so our emphasis was to improve the total process. As you will see later in the book, centering a process, or moving its average, is generally much easier than reducing its variation. Reducing a process variation often involves a complete change in the process, not just a minor adjustment.

If the problem definition indicates that the problem is large variation and that the centering of the process is not the issue, then you would have no choice but to try and identify the individual causes of the variation and try to reduce their effect.

Again, you will save yourself a lot of trouble if you can make the problem definition more specific than just stating that the variation is too high. Does the problem happen on a regular or spaced frequency? Is it related to shift, machine, product, operator, or day? Any specific information will dramatically reduce the number of different mini-populations from which you will have to gather samples and/or data. This more specific problem definition will then be compared to the related fishbone diagram to try to isolate the conditions that you must sample.

Process with Too Much Variation

Suppose our earlier ground-pin-diameter error had been defined as being periodic, affecting one machine at a time and not being a process off-center problem. Figure 13–6 shows the fishbone diagram with this new problem definition in mind.

Since the problem is defined as periodic, let's see which of these input variables would likely have a production-line time period associated with the problem. It appears that each KPIV (experience, grinding wheel wear and setup, gauge verification, and grinder maintenance) may have different time periods. With this insight, go back and see if it is possible to get even better problem definition that will allow us to focus more sharply on the specific problem.

Assume that you go back to the customer or whoever triggered the issue and find that the problem occurs every several weeks on each line but not on all lines at the same time. Let's look

FIGURE 13–6

Fishbone Diagram
Input Variables Affecting Pin Diameter Errors

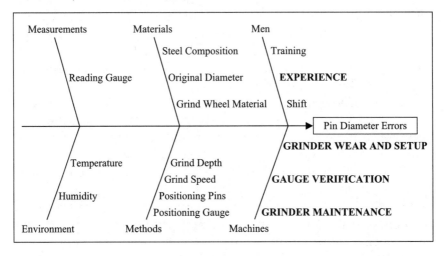

at our KPIVs with this in mind. Experience would be random, not every several weeks. The grinding wheels are replaced every several days, so the time period doesn't match. Simplified gauge verifications are done monthly, so that cycle also doesn't fit. However, grinder maintenance is done on a two-week cycle, one machine at a time. This variable fits the problem definition. We now need to run a controlled test.

We want to control everything other than grinder maintenance during our sample and/or data collection. We will change the grinding wheel frequently, verifying its setup to make sure that it is not an issue. We will have experienced people working on the process, and we will be sure that simplified gauge verification was done. All of these input variables were defined by the experts as being critical, so we want to be sure to have them in control.

We will use an experienced crew on the day shift, verifying that the pin and grinding wheel materials are correct, that the lathe is set up correctly (grinder depth and/or speed, position of pin and gauge), and that an experienced person will be doing the measurements. We will minimize the effects of temperature and humidity by taking samples and/or data at the same time each day. Since we don't know if the problem is caused by not performing grinder maintenance often enough or if the grinder takes some time to debug after maintenance, we probably want to take samples daily for at least two weeks to get a better idea of the actual cause.

As you can see in all the above examples, good problem definition combined with a fishbone diagram will focus us on what samples and/or data we need. The detail within the fishbone diagram will further help us make sure that the other variables in the process being measured are as stable as possible, with the exception of the variable being evaluated.

Once a change is implemented, samples and/or data must be collected to verify that the improvement actually happened. The same care must be taken in collecting samples and/or data validating the improvement as was taken during the problem-solving process. You can use quality department data for validation if the means of collecting data stays consistent before and after the change. If you can't trust the quality department data, you will have to use additional data samples.

IMPORTANCE OF GETTING GOOD SAMPLES AND DATA

Minimum sample sizes, simplified gauge verification, and statistical tests to validate significant change all play a part. But the sample and/or data collection must be right to start with so that you have data to analyze that are truly representative of the process you are checking.

While testing, collecting data, and validating the process improvement, you and others must be alert for any event that makes your conclusions suspicious. When in doubt, don't believe the results. Redo the test!

The use of good problem definition and the fishbone diagram to help decide what to sample is valid for many applications.

Sales managers, store salespeople, distribution center employees, and others can assist in making a fishbone diagram where the head of the fish is inaccurate sales forecasts. Just as in manufacturing, there are probably many influencing variables. The problem definition and fishbone diagram will help in deciding on the critical variables and in making sure that your sampling and data are focused and minimally affected by input variables other than the one you are testing.

Marketing folks can get advertising experts from newspapers, TV, and magazines to assist in making a fishbone where "ineffective advertising" is the head of the fish (problem). Variables may be advertising style, media type, frequency, market, and so on. This information assists in determining what and how to sample.

Software developers can get users to assist in making a fishbone diagram, with the head being software crashes. Output can be used to identify which areas to focus on to get data on each key cause of software crashes.

Everyone from sales to accounting can contribute to a fishbone diagram with too many overdue receivables as the head. Again, this is needed before determining what to sample to get good data on the problem.

Suppose an insurance company feels they have too many policies with only minor differences. A group of sales representatives and customers can make a fishbone diagram with the head being the excess of policies. Key causes will be identified and data can be collected based on the problem definition.

CHAPTER 13 REVIEW

1. Getting valid samples and data is just as important as applying any statistical tool.
2. The people and methods used for taking the samples and data affect the randomness and accuracy of both. Also, the product population is changing as the process changes, sometimes quite radically and often.
3. It is generally not possible to sample all the mini-populations caused by the people and changes caused by the process.
4. Use the fishbone diagram to identify the key process input variables (KPIVs) that cause all these mini-populations. Use the problem definition and close analysis of the fishbone diagram to limit your focus.

5. Generally, the easiest approach to improving a process's output quality is to center the total process rather than reducing the variation.

6. If the variation is very high, you may have no choice but to attempt to reduce it. Use a fishbone diagram to assist.

7. Take a statistically valid sample before and after a change to be confident that the improvement was significant.

8. Once the change is implemented, validate the effect on the total process. You can use quality department data for this validation if the means of collecting data stay consistent before and after the change. If you can't trust the quality department data, you will have to take additional samples.

Simplified Gauge Verification

What you will learn in this chapter is how to determine gauge error and how to correct this error if it is excessive. When a problem surfaces, one of the first things we have to do is check our data, especially the measurements. The issue of the accuracy, repeatability, and reproducibility of gauge readings crops up everywhere a variables data measurement (decimals) is taken. Simplified gauge verification is needed to make sure that gauge error is not excessive.

Before we use data, we must satisfy ourselves that the data are accurate. Data can give us a false sense of security when we do not know that the data are incorrect. We may believe that the process is in control and that we are making acceptable product. If our data are wrong, we could also make erroneous changes to the process.

One of the most frequent sources of measurement error is the device itself that is used to measure the product or process. This device can be as simple as a ruler or as complex as a radiation sensor. These errors can be compounded by the difference between the gauges used by the supplier and those used by the customer, or by variation among gauges within a manufacturing plant.

In Chapter 13 we stated that Six Sigma was concerned with how a product or process differed from the nominal case, that any error was due to a combination of the average product being off center plus any variation of the products around that average.

A gauge used to measure a product can have similar issues: The average gauge reading can be off center from the true dimension, and variations can occur within the gauge readings. For any product of a known dimension, all of the individuals within a group of people measuring that product with a particular gauge will get an error. That error may be small, but they will get an error. That error will be a combination of the average reading being different than the actual product dimension and a range of measurements around the average reading. Figure 14–1 is a visual representation of a possible set of readings taken on one part. In this case the readings all happen to be greater than the true part dimension.

Figure 14–1 shows the actual gauge readings. *Gauge error* is defined as the difference among the various gauge readings versus a nominal part's true dimension and its allowable tolerance.

In Six Sigma projects, the use of the simplified gauge verification tool often gives insight that allows for big gains with no additional efforts. In the DMAIC process, this tool can be used in the Define, Measure, Analyze, Improve, and Control steps.

FIGURE 14–1

Gauge Reading on a Product of a Known Dimension

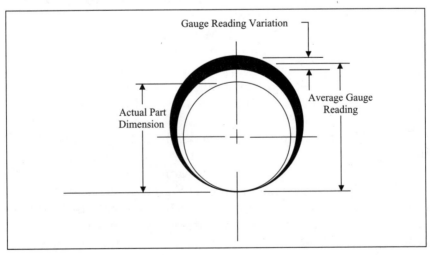

TIP

The Maximum Allowable Gauge Error: 30 Percent of the Tolerance

Ideally a gauge should not use up more than 10 percent of the tolerance. The maximum allowable gauge error generally used is 30 percent.

If a gauge has a 30 percent error, then the supplier must keep the product measurements within 70 percent of the tolerance to ensure that the product is within specification.

Some plants discover that as many as half of their gauges will not pass the 30 percent maximum error criteria. Even after extensive rework many gauges cannot pass the simplified gauge verification because the part tolerance is too tight for the gauge design.

Since most plants do not want to run with reduced in-house tolerances, a problem gauge must be upgraded to "use up" less of the tolerance.

CHECKING FOR GAUGE ERROR

There are several methods of checking for gauge error. The method discussed in this book emphasizes improving the gauge (when required) rather than retraining inspectors. Inspectors change frequently, and it is nearly impossible to get someone to routinely follow a very critical procedure to get a gauge reading accurately. It is better to have a robust gauge that is not likely to be used incorrectly.

Simplified gauge verification includes both *repeatability/ reproducibility* and *accuracy*. In simple terms, it checks for both the variations in gauge readings and for the correctness of the average gauge reading. Figure 14–2 gives a visual representation of simplified gauge verification.

DEFINITIONS

repeatability/reproducibility   These terms relate to consistencies in readings from a gauge. *Repeatability* is the consistency of an individual's gauge readings, and *reproducibility* is the consistency of two or more people's readings from that same gauge. Simplified gauge verification combines the two.

accuracy   *Accuracy* relates to the correctness of the average of all the gauge readings versus some agreed-upon true measurement value.

TIP

Generate masters for simplified gauge verification.

Simplified gauge verification requires the identification of several "master" products near the product's specification center. The supplier and customer must agree on the dimensions of these masters.

Masters can be quantified by using outside firms that have calibrated specialized measuring devices or by getting mutual agreement between the supplier and customer.

FIGURE 14–2

Visual Representation of Simplified Gauge Verification

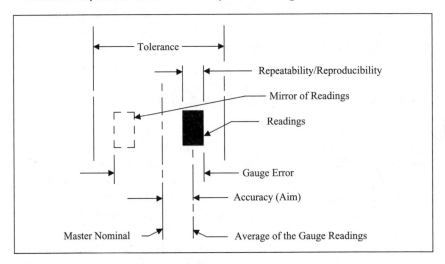

The reason the gauge error includes plus or minus the accuracy plus the repeatability/reproducibility is that the tolerance, which is the reference, also includes any allowable plus-or-minus variation on both sides of the process center. This makes the ratio comparison with the tolerance valid.

INSTRUCTIONS FOR SIMPLIFIED GAUGE VERIFICATIONS

Using a randomly picked master, have three different inspectors (or operators) measure the master 7 times each. Have them measure the product in a fashion similar to what they would do in

---

FORMULA

Simplified Gauge Verification, Variables Data

$$\text{Percent gauge error } = \frac{5s + 2 * |\text{master} - \bar{x}|}{\text{tolerance}} * 100 \text{ percent}$$

(Ideally < 10 percent; max 30 percent)

$\bar{x}$ = average of *all* 21 readings of a master product
s = standard deviation of *all* 21 readings of the master product
Master = standardized dimension of the master product
Tolerance = allowable product tolerance (maximum − minimum)
$|\text{Master} - \bar{x}|$ = accuracy or aim, ignoring minus signs

---

normal production (amount of time, method, and so on). Calculate the average $\bar{x}$ and standard deviation s of *all* 21 readings. If the standard deviation s is calculated on a manual calculator, use the $n - 1$ option if it's available.

Just for reference, the reason the s is multiplied by 5 in the formula is that ±2.5 sigma represents 99 percent of the items on a normal distribution. This means that the formula is indicative of the maximum error that would be expected on 99 percent of the products.

If two times the accuracy $|\text{master} - \bar{x}|$ is the predominant error (compared to the total gauge error), you should examine the setup procedure for the gauge, specifically the nominal setting. It is normally easier to reduce gauge accuracy error than repeatability/reproducibility error. Adjusting the gauge setup will often correct gauge inaccuracy.

We chose to use a master that was close to the center of the specification, which is sufficient in most cases. However, for some types of optical gauges, you need to verify readings at both the center and at an end of the specification because mechanical movement of the optics can cause them to read correctly at the center but not at the end. In most cases, however, masters at the center are sufficient.

TIP

Document simplified gauge verification.

Gauge verification must be set up as a regular routine, and documentation of the readings must be kept.

The simplified gauge verification is in addition to (and independent of) any quality department gauge setup procedure, which is done separately by trained people taking whatever time is required.

Example of Simplified Gauge Verification on Bearings

We want to perform the simplified gauge verification procedure to test the gauge we are using to measure the diameters on bearings. We have established a master bearing, which is near nominal. We will now have three inspectors (or operators) measure this master bearing 7 times each. Here are the results:

Master bearing standardized reading = 1.0004 inches

Allowable bearing dimensions: Max = 1.0050 inches

Min = 0.9960 inch

Therefore,

Tolerance = 0.0090 inch

Inspector	Reading No.	Dimension, Inches
A	1	1.0018
	2	1.0001
	3	0.9998
	4	1.0011
	5	0.9996
	6	1.0001
	7	1.0001
B	1	0.9992
	2	1.0011
	3	1.0002
	4	0.9991
	5	1.0004
	6	0.9988
	7	1.001
C	1	0.9997
	2	0.9988
	3	1.0008
	4	1.0015
	5	0.9998
	6	1.0006
	7	0.9996

Average $\bar{x}$ = 1.000152 inches

Standard deviation s = 0.000851 inch

$5s$ = 0.004253 inch

$$\text{Percent gauge error} = \frac{5s + 2*|\text{master} - \bar{x}|}{\text{tolerance}} * 100 \text{ percent}$$

$$= \frac{0.0043 + 2*|1.0004 - 1.0002|}{0.0090} * 100 \text{ percent}$$

$$= 52 \text{ percent}$$

Since the calculated gauge error of 52 percent exceeds the allowable 30 percent, we must go back and rework or recalibrate the gauge. Assume we rework the gauge. Here are the new results:

Gauge Readings after Rework
Master bearing standardized reading = 1.0004 inches
Allowable bearing dimensions: Max = 1.0050 inches
Min = 0.9960 inch

Therefore,

Tolerance = 0.0090 inch

Inspector	Reading No.	Dimension, Inches
A	1	1.0008
	2	1.0006
	3	1.0001
	4	1.0011
	5	1.0004
	6	0.9998
	7	1.0007
B	1	0.9996
	2	0.9999
	3	1.001
	4	1.0005
	5	1.0001
	6	1.0003
	7	1.0002
C	1	1.0007
	2	1.0006
	3	0.9996
	4	0.9999
	5	1.0004
	6	1.0006
	7	1.0003

$$\text{Average } \bar{x} = 1.000343 \text{ inches}$$
$$\text{Standard deviation } s = 0.000426 \text{ inch}$$
$$5s = 0.002131 \text{ inch}$$

$$\text{Percent gauge error} = \frac{5s + 2 * |\text{master} - \bar{x}|}{\text{tolerance}} * 100 \text{ percent}$$

$$= \frac{0.0021 + 0.0001}{0.0090} * 100 \text{ percent} = 24.4 \text{ percent}$$

Although the calculated gauge error of 24.4 percent is not great, it is acceptable. Note that by just looking at the raw readings before and after rework, it is not obvious whether the gauge is doing an acceptable job, even when reading a master bearing with a known diameter. That is why simplified gauge verification often yields a great payback—because problems (or opportunities) from gauges are often hidden.

Case Study: Gauge Error on Measuring Nonflatness

It is important that the rim of this particular product be flat because in an assembly operation it will be "sealed" to another part. Flatness is important to get a good seal.

Nonflatness was an ongoing problem on this product. The nonflatness was measured by inspecting a sample of products using "feeler gauges" of various thicknesses. The thickest feeler gauge that could be inserted between the product rim and a flat plate determined the nonflatness.

This was a difficult measurement because not only was there a lot of judgment as to when a feeler gauge began to "drag" but also it was difficult to do this measurement without tilting the product. Since in the assembly operation the product was sitting with no sideways force, just gravity holding it down, tilting the product was not consistent with the way the product was actually used.

TIP

Take advantage of simplified gauge verification.

If you have any gauges that take critical measurements and simplified gauge verification has not been done, you have a real opportunity to make a substantial improvement. This is especially true if the customer has reported any problems related to the product or if quality losses are high.

It was difficult to even get enough agreement on "real" nonflatness measurements to develop masters because of the difficulty of taking this measurement. Finally, a laboratory optical gauge was used to measure the nonflatness without putting a tilting force on the product. Only then was it possible to develop master products to do the simplified gauge verification. The feeler gauge method of measuring nonflatness failed the simplified gauge verification dramatically.

A production version of the optical gauge was then designed, and that enabled the plant to successfully measure the nonflatness.

GAUGE R&R

Most Six Sigma classes teach a process called *gauge R&R* to check gauges. This method addresses only repeatability and reproducibility, not accuracy (aim). Gauge R&R uses current production products rather than masters. To get valid gauge R&R test results, the current production products must include the full range of process dimensions, which are not always readily available. If the test samples do not include the full range of process dimensions, the gauge R&R often will not pass.

The gauge R&R output is given as an *analysis of variance* (ANOVA), a rather sophisticated mathematical method that allows for the separation of gauge error into operator, gauge, and part contribution. The idea in gauge R&R is that, if the operator is the key contributor to the gauge error, then retraining or taking the person off the job will correct the problem. If the part is the biggest contributor to the error, it means that something about the physical part, such as distortion, is causing the issue; no direction is given for resolving this. If the gauge is the biggest contributor, then the gauge has to be replaced or repaired.

In gauge R&R, accuracy is not tested. There is no attempt to check the combined error of repeatability/reproducibility and accuracy. In fact, gauge R&R doesn't directly address accuracy (aim) at all. It is up to the user of the gauge R&R method to find a way to estimate the total effect of any repeatability/reproducibility error and accuracy error.

Simplified gauge verification combines repeatability/reproducibility and accuracy into one test and emphasizes total gauge error. This emphasis is based on much experience (frustration) in the difficulty of getting a changing group of inspectors to follow precise instructions on taking measurements. The gauge must be designed for ease of use so that the operator error is minor and included as part of the total gauge error. Also, the part contribution of gauge error can't be addressed separately in any case, so why separate it?

Anyone choosing not to use the simplified gauge verification should consider the traditional gauge R&R because both will give benefits. If gauge R&R is used, accuracy will have to be checked separately, and some estimate of the total effect of accuracy and variation will have to be made by the user. Obviously, I believe that simplified gauge verification is a better choice.

CHAPTER 14 REVIEW

1. In the DMAIC process, simplified gauge verification can be used in the Define, Measure, Analyze, Improve, and Control steps.
2. Ideally a gauge should not use up more than 10 percent of the allowable tolerance. The maximum allowed is generally 30 percent.
3. The first step in simplified gauge verification is to get one or more master products near the specification center. The supplier and customer must agree on the dimensions of these masters. In some types of gauges (optical), you need to verify readings at both the center and at an end of the specification. But most gauges need masters only at the center of the tolerance.
4. Some production plants discover that as many as half of their gauges will not meet the criterion of maximum 30 percent of tolerance.
5. Emphasize improving the gauge (when required) rather than retraining inspectors. Inspectors come and go, so having them do a complex or detailed inspection process is not a good long-term solution.
6. The simplified gauge verification formula includes both repeatability/reproducibility (ability to duplicate a reading) and accuracy (aim, or correctness of average reading).

7. Simplified gauge verification must be set up as a regular routine, and documentation must be kept.

8. Gauge R&R, another approach to verifying that a gauge is not using excessive amounts of the tolerance, is an alternate method. However, it checks for repeatability/reproducibility only. It does not include error due to inaccuracy, so the user must estimate the combined effect of repeatability/reproducibility and accuracy error.

Basic Probability and Plotting

Ignoti nulla cupido.   (The unknown does not tempt.)

—Latin saying

Part Four, which includes Chapters 15 and 16, reviews basic probability and the importance of plotting data.

Much Six Sigma work can't be done without some understanding of probability and statistics.

Plotting data is a needed step in implementing many of the Six Sigma tools. Plotted data often give insights that can't be discovered with any numerical test.

CHAPTER 15

Probability

What you will learn in this chapter is to let data drive problem solving. However, to interpret data, you need to make a judgment as to whether unusual results were due to a *random cause*—for example, someone is flipping a coin and getting an excessive number of heads by chance—or due to an *assignable cause*—for example, someone is flipping a coin that has two heads. Knowledge of probability assists you in making this determination with a minimum number of samples (coin flips in this example).

Many of the tools discussed in the coming chapters require some basic understanding of probability and statistics. You will be able to use the included review of probability to solve many problems in the workplace without using any additional Six Sigma tools.

Often data you want to analyze will have some related probability that can assist. For example, if you have a manufactured part with four sides and a defect is always on one side, understanding probability could help you find the defect cause. If 14 people are taking phone orders but more than 1/14th of the errors are from one person, you may want to find out why. If there are eight salespeople but one salesperson is generating 25 percent of the total sales, you may want to get the other salespeople to emulate the best salesperson. However, you first have to be sure that all of the above-observed results are not due to just random chance but instead are truly indicative of a real difference.

Probability

Manufacturing
On any production line with multiple heads, compare defect levels from each head to see if they are significantly different. Compare production lines, shifts, defects on different days of the week, and so on. Often you will see significant differences that can be addressed at little cost.

Sales
Compare the productivity of the company's salespeople. The criteria could include new customers and sales. Cross training between the best and worst performers can often improve both. Also, through these careful comparisons compensation can be made more equitable.

Marketing
Check if sales increased significantly after a marketing campaign.

Accounting and Software Development
Compare error incidence for significant difference between groups.

Receivables
Check the effect of increased or decreased monitoring of overdue receivables.

Insurance
Compare the complaints at different treatment centers. The criteria could include patient care and billing errors.

In the course of our daily lives, we frequently make estimates on the likelihood of an event or its probability. Examples are the chance of rain, winning the lottery, or being in a plane crash. Some probabilities are easy to calculate and intuit, like figuring the chance of getting a head on a coin flip (1 in 2, or 0.5). Some probabilities are not easy to calculate or intuit, like the probability of an earthquake.

In Six Sigma we also need to make an estimate of the probability of an event. In this way we can make some judgment as to whether something just happened due to random coincidence or due to an assignable cause that we should address. Luckily the work you will be doing probably does *not* involve earthquakes!

We will start with problems where we know the mathematical probability of a single random event, and we will use *Excel*'s BINOMDIST to get an answer.

DEFINITIONS

n   This variable represents the number of independent trials, like the number of coin tosses or the number of parts measured.

probability *p* (or probability *s*)   This is the probability of a success on *each individual trial*, like the likelihood of a head on 1 coin flip or a defect on 1 part. This is always a proportion and generally shown as a decimal, like 0.0156.

number *s* (or *x* successes)   This is the total number of successes that you are looking for, like getting exactly 3 heads.

probability *P*   This is the probability of getting a given number of successes from <u>all</u> *the trials*, like the probability of 3 heads in 5 coin tosses or 14 defects in a shipment of 1,000 parts. This is often the answer to the problem.

cumulative   This is the sum of the probabilities of getting the *number of successes or less*, like getting 3 *or less* heads on 5 flips of a coin. This option is used on *Less-than* and *More-than problems*.

Problem 1

What are the chances of getting exactly 2 heads in 3 flips of a coin?

We will solve this using *Excel*. After bringing up the *Excel* worksheet, click the Paste function or the Insert function in the toolbar. Under Category, click on Statistical. Then, under Function, click on BINOMDIST.

In the first box, enter the Number of successes (number of heads) you want in these trials, which is 2. The second box asks for the Number of trials, which is 3. The third box asks for the probability of a Success (head) on each trial, which is 0.5.

The fourth box asks if the problem requires the cumulative probability. If you answer True, you get the sum of the probabilities up to and including 2 (the probability of zero heads plus the probability of 1 head plus the probability of 2 heads), which is the probability of getting 2 or less heads. In this problem you do *not* want the cumulative probability, so answer False. You then get our desired probability of exactly 2 heads, which is $P = 0.375$.

Here is a summary of what we just did:

Excel **BINOMDIST**
Number of successes = 2
Trials = 3
Probability = 0.5
Cumulative: false

The result is $P = 0.375$.

TIP

Use the sum of probabilities = 1.
    Since the sum of the probabilities of all possible outcomes always equals 1, we can often use this knowledge to simplify a problem.
    For example, if we want to know the probability of getting 1 or more heads on 10 coin tosses, we can find the probability of getting zero heads, then subtract this probability from 1. This is much easier than adding the probabilities of 1 head + 2 heads + 3 heads + 4 heads + 5 heads + 6 heads + 7 heads + 8 heads + 9 heads + 10 heads.

Problem 2
What is the probability of getting 2 or less heads in 3 flips of a coin?

We will show three ways to solve this problem.
    Using the BINOMDIST in *Excel*, you can do it three times, adding the results of zero, 1, and 2 successes (with Cumulative false), and you get $0.125 + 0.375 + 0.375 = 0.875$.
    Or you can recognize that the only outcome that has more than 2 heads is 3 heads. Using *Excel*'s BINOMDIST, we find that the probability of 3 heads is 0.125. Since the sum of the probabilities of all possible outcomes always equals 1, we can subtract the probability of 3 heads (0.125) from 1 to get the answer, which is 0.875.
    The following is the most direct way to the answer. Using *Excel* BINOMDIST, we can realize that the Cumulative true gives the probability of getting 2 or less heads, which is what we want. So here's how we can get the answer directly:

Don't use the cumulative function for the probability of a single outcome or success, like 3 heads out of 5 coin tosses. Enter False in the box for cumulative function.

Use the cumulative function for Less than, Equal to or less than, Equal to or more than, or More than a given outcome or success, as follows.

For Less than a given outcome, like less than 3 heads out of 8 coin tosses, use the cumulative function True with the success at 1 *less than* the given value $(3 - 1 = 2)$:

Success $= 2$

Trials $= 8$

$p = 0.5$

Cumulative: true

The result is $P = 0.1445$.

For Equal to or less than a given outcome, like 3 heads or less out of 8 coin tosses, use the cumulative function True with the success at the given value (3):

Success $= 3$

Trials $= 8$

$p = 0.5$

Cumulative: true

The result is $P = 0.3633$.

For More than a given outcome, like more than 3 heads out of 8 coin tosses, use the cumulative function True with the success at the given value (3); then subtract the result from 1:

Success $= 3$

Trials $= 8$

$p = 0.5$

Cumulative: true

The result is 0.3633. P would then equal $1.0000 - 0.3633 = 0.6367$.

For Equal to or more than a given outcome, like 3 or more heads out of 8 coin tosses, use the cumulative function True with the success at 1 *less than* the given outcome $(3 - 1 = 2)$; then subtract the result from 1:

Success $= 2$

Trials $= 8$

$p = 0.5$

Cumulative: true

The result is 0.1445. P would then equal $1.0000 - 0.1445 = 0.8555$.

Excel **BINOMDIST**
Number of successes = 2
Trials = 3
$p = 0.5$
Cumulative: true

The result is $P = 0.875$.

TIP

Independent trials are not affected by earlier results.

The probability on an independent trial is *not* affected by results on earlier trials. For example, someone could have flipped 10 heads in a row, but the probability of a head on the next coin flip is still $p = 0.5$ assuming both the coin and the person tossing it are honest, and so on.

Problem 3

What is the chance of getting 7 or less tails on 10 flips of a coin?

Excel **BINOMDIST**
Successes = 7
Trials = 10
$p = 0.5$
Cumulative: true

The result is $P = 0.9453$.

Problem 4

What are the chances of getting at least 7 tails on 10 coin flips?

Using the *Excel* BINOMDIST and realizing that the chance of at least 7 tails (or 7 or more tails) is the same as 1 minus the chance of 6 or less tails, we solve as follows:

Excel **BINOMDIST**
Successes = 6
Trials = 10
$p = 0.5$
Cumulative: true

The result is 0.8281. *P* would then equal $1.0000 - 0.8281 = 0.1719$, or 17.19 percent.

Problem 5

A vendor is making 12.5 percent defective product. In a box of 10 random parts from this vendor, what is the probability of finding 2 or less defects?

> ### *Excel* **BINOMDIST**
> Success = 2
> Trials = 10
> $p = 0.125$
> Cumulative: true

The result is $P = 0.880$, or 88.0 percent.

Problem 6

A salesperson has been losing 30 percent of potential sales. In a study of 10 random sales contacts from this salesperson, what is the probability of finding 3 or more successful sales?

We must be careful that what we call a "success" (*successful* sales in this case) is consistent with the rest of the problem statement (which is currently stated as the percentage of *lost* sales). We can restate the question as "getting 70 percent of potential sales" so the success is measured in the same terms as rest of the problem statement. Then we have the following problem.

A salesperson has been successful in getting 70 percent of potential sales. In a study of 10 random sales contacts from this salesperson, what is the probability of finding 3 or more successful sales?

Again, to save work, we know that "3 or more successful sales" is the same as 1 minus the probability of "2 or less successful sales":

> ### *Excel* **BINOMDIST**
> Success = 2
> Trials = 10
> $p = 0.70$
> Cumulative: true

The result is 0.0016. P would then equal $1.0000 - 0.0016 = 0.9984$, or 99.84 percent.

Case Study: Most Defects from One Machine

A product had a hole stamped by one of two machines. These machines also stamped an identification mark on the product so that someone could identify which machine stamped the hole. A quality engineer randomly collected 80 parts with defective holes. He examined them and found that 49 defects were from one of the two machines. He concluded that there was less than a 3 percent chance that 49 or more defects out of 80 would be coming from one machine due to random cause alone.

So he went looking for anything suspect on the machine that was making most of the defects. He found that the fixture that held the product on the machine had a burr on one side, causing the product to be slightly out of line while the hole was being punched. He had the machine operator use a hand grinder to remove the burr, and the product then seated properly.

The engineer then rechecked another random 80 defective holes and this time found no significant difference between the two machines.

Let's see if we agree with the engineer's conclusion that the higher number of defects coming from one machine was probably not due to random cause alone. ("Random" would mean that there was nothing peculiar about this machine: he just happened to get a sample with more defects from one machine.) Note that he checked the chances of 49 *or more* defects happening randomly because there was nothing special about being *exactly* 49.

Excel BINOMDIST

Successes = 48

Trials = 80

$p = 0.5$ (1/2, the probability of the defect randomly coming from one machine)

Cumulative: true

The result is 0.9717. P would then equal $1.0000 - 0.9717 = 0.0283$, or 2.83 percent.

TIP

Maximum 1,000 Trials in *Excel* BINOMDIST

Excel BINOMDIST allows a maximum of 1,000 trials. So if you have more than 1,000 trials, proportion the trials and number of successes to 1,000.

For example, if the data consist of 2,000 trials and you are looking for 140 successes, use *Excel* BINOMDIST with 1,000 trials and 70 successes. The p is not affected.

So there is only a 2.83 percent chance of getting 49 or more of the 80 defects from one machine due to random results. So the engineer was right to be suspicious—and his conclusion enabled him to focus his attention on the one machine, which minimized the areas he had to examine to identify the problem source.

Problem 7

These are the results of 109 random erroneous orders processed by 7 telephone operators, A through G:

Operator	Erroneous Orders
A	14
B	15
C	23
D	13
E	16
F	15
G	13

Is Operator C's performance worse than we should expect since C's 23-error total is higher than that of the other 6 operators? We would want to be at least 95 percent confident that the performance was poor before any action was taken.

We want to check against the likelihood of getting 23 *or more* errors, rather than exactly 23. This will be more conservative, and it's not important that there are *exactly* 23 order errors:

Excel **BINOMDIST**
Successes = 22
Trials = 109
$p = 1/7 = 0.14286$ (random chance since there are 7 operators)
Cumulative: true

The result is 0.9662. P would then equal $1.0000 - 0.9662 = 0.0338$, or 3.38 percent.

This means that there is a 3.4 percent chance of this happening randomly without an assignable cause. The confidence level of the conclusion that this is not random would therefore be $100 - 3.4 = 96.6$ percent, which is more than the 95 percent test threshold.

Therefore, we can conclude with a 95 percent confidence that Operator C is performing worse than what would be expected. Of course, the reason for the poorer performance could be something as simple as the operator being new on the job.

Note that when checking for significant differences when you have a large number of possibilities (there are 7 operators in the above group), the odds increase that at least 1 will be significantly different than the others. That is not unlike comparing 2 operators multiple times. If you do enough comparisons, you will eventually get a sample that shows significant difference. That is why you never want to overreact to the outcome of one sample, especially if the other variables are not being controlled.

CHAPTER 15 REVIEW

1. Six Sigma work can't be done without some understanding of probability and statistics.
2. Letting data drive your problem solving will often save work and lead to a condensed list of solution considerations.
3. Using basic probability techniques on the data will help separate random results from assignable causes.
4. Since the sum of the probabilities of all possible outcomes always equals 1, we can often use this knowledge to simplify a problem.
5. *Excel* BINOMDIST is sufficient for doing the probability calculations, using the cumulative function to save work in doing Less-than or More-than calculations.
6. Examine the data carefully to make sure they are truly independent.
7. Although probability techniques help to focus on solution options, usually additional analysis or trials are needed to identify a specific cause-and-effect relationship.
8. Because our confidence level is *never* 100 percent, any change must be verified with future tests or data. Past data can never completely validate a change.
9. You can already do real Six Sigma work by applying these basic probability techniques. *Even if you read no further in this book, just applying this and the techniques presented in earlier chapters will enable you to make substantial and meaningful improvements in diverse applications.*

Data Plots and Distributions

What you will learn in this chapter is to plot data and to spot opportunities from these plots. You will also learn what a "normal" distribution of data is and some terminology to describe this distribution. This understanding will help you to solve many real problems and to do Six Sigma work. Plotting data is a needed step in implementing many of the Six Sigma tools. It is used in all of the steps of the DMAIC methodology.

Using Charts (Histograms) and the Normal Distribution on Real Problems

Manufacturing
Make histograms on processes, plants, and/or shifts that are supposed to be the same and you may find differences.

Sales
Use histogram charts to compare sales results by year, by month, or by sales office. You can also compare success in getting new customers or graph additional sales generated per travel dollar.

Marketing
Look at market segments per month and compare changes year to year with marketing campaigns or dollars spent on advertising.

Accounting and Software Development
Use histogram charts to graphically compare employees versus lines of code written or accounting forms completed. Accounting and software groups are very visually oriented, and they relate well to data presented in charts this way.

Receivables
Plot the monthly receivables year over year, and then compare that graph to the cash flow graph.

Insurance
Compare surgeries done in comparable hospitals to spot cost differences.

NORMAL DATA

A lathe is machining shafts to a 1.0000-inch nominal diameter. You carefully measure 100 diameters of these shafts. If you sort the diameters into 0.0005-inch-wide "bins" and plot these data, you will get a *histogram* similar to that shown in Figure 16–1. In this illustration, the ends of the shafts are shown for clarity. These would not be shown in a regular histogram.

> **TIP**
>
> In a histogram, assume no values are on bin "edges."
>
> When a value appears to be exactly on a bin edge, convention is to put that value into the higher bin. In Figure 16–1, if a shaft were measured to be *exactly* 1.0000 inch, it would be put into the 1.0000- to 1.0005-inch bin.
>
> Not having a value on a bin edge is not difficult to accept when you consider that with an accurate enough measurement system, you would be able to see even the smallest difference from exactly 1.0000 inch.

We must now interpret the data shown in this histogram. First, notice that the process is centered and that the left half is a mirror image of the right. What percent of the shafts are within 0.001 inch of the 1.000-inch nominal diameter? Adding the bin quantities on both sides of the center ±0.001 inch, we get 68, or 68 percent of the shafts. It will be shown later that on any process with a normal distribution, this 0.68 point (or 0.34 on either side of the center) is equal to ±1 sigma (or ±1 standard deviation).

For illustration purposes, 1 sigma in this case just happens to equal 0.001 inch. Therefore, 2 sigma = 0.002 inch. What percentage of the shafts are within ±2 sigma of the nominal diameter? Again, counting the bin quantities within ±0.002 inch on both sides of the center, we find that 96 shafts, or 96 percent of the shafts, are within 2 sigma of the nominal diameter.

> **TIP**
> Reference Data within a Normal Distribution
>
> It is handy to remember that approximately 2/3 (68 percent) of the data points are within ±1 sigma of the center in a process with a normal distribution and that 95 percent are within ±2 sigma. Another good reference number is that 99.7 percent of the data points are within ±3 sigma of the center.

FIGURE 16-1

Histogram of 100 Shafts
1-Inch Nominal Shafts Sorted into 0.0005-Inch-Wide Bins

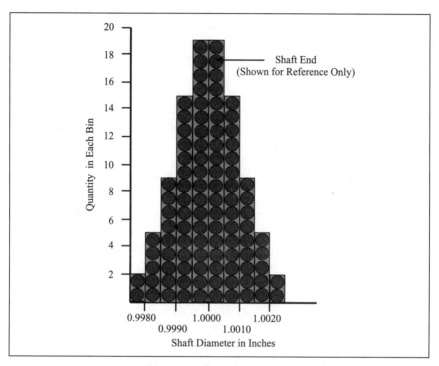

All of the preceding discussion referred to data on both sides of the center. However, it is often important to know what is occurring on only one end of the data. For example, what percent of the shafts are at least 1 sigma greater than 1.0000 inch in diameter? Adding the bin quantities to the right of +1 sigma (sigma in this case happens to be +0.0010 inch), we get 16, or 16 percent.

We will be using charts (and computer programs) that take the reference points at the center or at either end of the data. You have to look carefully at the data and chart illustration to see what reference point is being used.

Now, using some of the techniques from the previous chapter on probability and assuming independence (assume you put the first shaft back before picking the second), what is the likelihood of randomly picking 2 shafts that are above 1.0000 inch in diameter? Since the probability of each is 0.5, the probability of 2 in a row is $0.5 \times 0.5 = 0.25$.

The preceding example used shafts, but other items could have been plotted with similar results. The height of 16-year-old boys could have been plotted, with the bins representing 1-inch height increments. Points scored by a basketball team could be shown as a histogram, with each bin representing 5 points. Clerical errors could be displayed, with each bin being an increment of errors per 10,000 entries. In all of those cases, you would probably get a normal distribution.

Let's now plot the same population of shaft data using 1,000 shafts and breaking the data into 0.0001-inch-wide bins, as shown in Figure 16–2.

As we get more data from this process and use smaller bins, the shape of the histogram approaches a *normal* distribution. In fact, it helps to think of a normal curve as a normal distribution with very small bins. This is the shape that will occur on many processes. Figure 16–3 shows how a normal distribution curve varies with different values of sigma.

TIP

Specifying a Normal Distribution

All that is needed to define a normal distributed set of data is the mean (average) and the standard deviation (sigma).

We could calculate the standard deviation (sigma) values manually, but since most $10 calculators and many computer programs do this so easily, we will not manually calculate them. If you use a calculator to calculate sigma and it gives you a choice of using n or $(n-1)$, use $(n-1)$.

Just for reference, here's the formula to solve for the standard deviation s on a set of n values, where $\bar{x}$ is the average of all the data points x:

$$s = \sqrt{\frac{(x_1 - \bar{x})^2 + (x_2 - \bar{x})^2 + \cdots + (x_n - \bar{x})^2}{n-1}}$$

The standard deviation is a measure of the spread of the normal curve. The greater the sigma, the more distributed the data with more highs and lows.

FIGURE 16–2

Histogram of 1,000 Shafts
1-Inch Nominal Shafts Sorted into 0.0001-Inch-Wide Bins

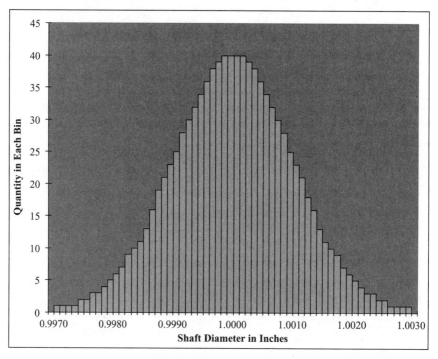

The use of normal curve standardized data allows us to make predictions on processes with normal distributions using small samples rather than our having to collect large samples for plotting hundreds of data points. As you will see later, once we establish that a process has a normal distribution, we can assume that this distribution will stay normal unless a major process change occurs.

We will be making a lot of analyses based on the likelihood of randomly finding data beyond ±2 sigma or outside of the expected 95 percent of the data. The case of our 1,000 shafts is depicted in the histogram shown in Figure 16–4 with this 5 percent area darkly shaded on the two ends below 0.9980 inch and above 1.0020 inch.

F I G U R E   16–3

Normal Distributions with Various Sigma Values

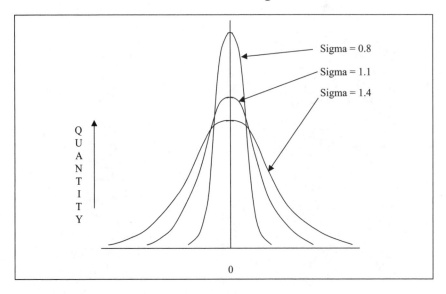

F I G U R E   16–4

Histogram of 1,000 Shafts with 5 Percent Shaded
1-Inch Nominal Shafts Sorted into 0.0001-Inch-Wide Bins

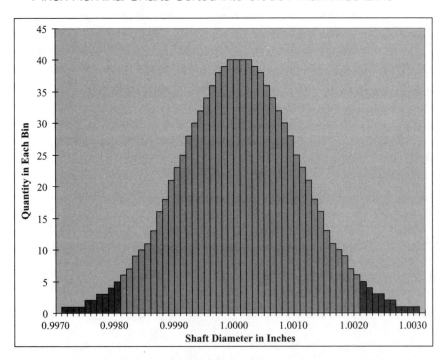

Figure 16–5 shows what this kind of distribution would look like if it were distributed randomly. The figure shows several hundred shafts with 5 percent of the shafts shaded. If you randomly picked a shaft from the distribution in Figure 16–5, you would be unlikely to pick a shaded one. In fact, if you picked a shaded shaft very often, you would probably begin to wonder if the distribution really had only 5 percent shaded shafts. Much of the analysis we will be making is based on similar logic.

Let's pursue this further. Suppose you had been led to believe that a distribution had only 5 percent shaded shafts, but you suspected that this was not true. If you picked 1 shaft randomly and it was shaded, you would be suspicious because you know that the chance of this happening randomly is only 5 percent. If you picked 2 shaded shafts in a row (assuming that you had put the first shaft back, mixed the shafts, and then randomly picked the second shaft), then you would *really* wonder since you know that the chance of randomly picking 2 shaded shafts in this manner is only $0.05 \times 0.05 = 0.0025$, or only 0.25 percent! From this limited sample, you would suspect that the whole shaft population was more than 5 percent shaded.

FIGURE 16–5

Random Shafts with 5 Percent Shaded

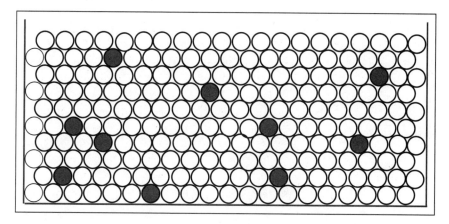

Z VALUE

The Standardized Normal Distribution Table in Figure 16–6 is one source of probability values to use on any normal process or set of data. The Z in the table refers to the number of sigma to the right of the center. The probabilities refer to the area to the right of the Z point.

Be aware that some tables (and computer programs) use different reference points, so examine tables and computer programs carefully before using them. Satisfy yourself that you can find data points on the Standardized Normal Distribution Table (Figure 16–6) relating to the previous shaft histogram with 0.0001-inch-wide bins (Figure 16–2).

So there is no confusion reading this table, let's be sure that it agrees with our reference number of ⅔ (68 percent) of data points being within ±1 sigma. Looking at the table, with $Z = 1.00$ (which means a sigma of 1), we get $P = 0.1587$, or approximately 0.16. This is illustrated in Figure 16–7. The left side is a mirror image of the right, as shown in Figure 16–8.

Given that the area under the curve always equals 1 (the sum of all the probabilities equals 1), we know that the white area under the curve equals 1 minus the shaded tails:

$$1 - (16 \text{ percent} + 16 \text{ percent}) = 1 - 32 \text{ percent} = 68 \text{ percent}$$

This confirms our reference number of 68 percent (or ⅔, which is easy to remember).

Problem 1
In the shaft process previously discussed, what is the probability of finding a shaft at least 2 sigma (0.0020 inch) over 1.000 inch in diameter? (*Note:* The Z value is an indication of how many sigma, so in this case $Z = 2$.)

Looking at the Standardized Normal Distribution Table in Figure 16–6, $Z = 2$, $P = 0.02275$.

Answer
$$P = 0.02275, \text{ or } 2.28 \text{ percent}$$

FIGURE 16–6

Standardized Normal Distribution Table

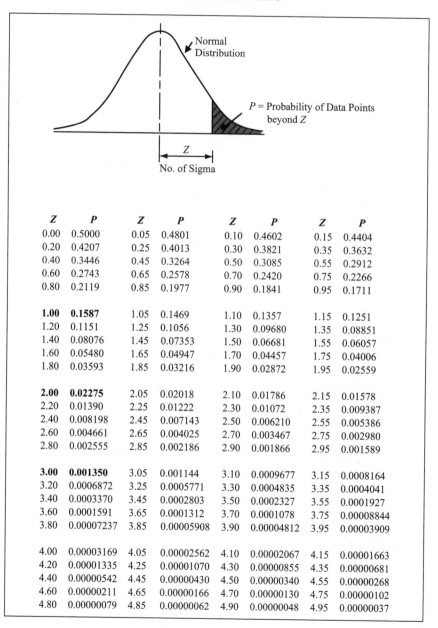

Z	P	Z	P	Z	P	Z	P
0.00	0.5000	0.05	0.4801	0.10	0.4602	0.15	0.4404
0.20	0.4207	0.25	0.4013	0.30	0.3821	0.35	0.3632
0.40	0.3446	0.45	0.3264	0.50	0.3085	0.55	0.2912
0.60	0.2743	0.65	0.2578	0.70	0.2420	0.75	0.2266
0.80	0.2119	0.85	0.1977	0.90	0.1841	0.95	0.1711
1.00	**0.1587**	1.05	0.1469	1.10	0.1357	1.15	0.1251
1.20	0.1151	1.25	0.1056	1.30	0.09680	1.35	0.08851
1.40	0.08076	1.45	0.07353	1.50	0.06681	1.55	0.06057
1.60	0.05480	1.65	0.04947	1.70	0.04457	1.75	0.04006
1.80	0.03593	1.85	0.03216	1.90	0.02872	1.95	0.02559
2.00	**0.02275**	2.05	0.02018	2.10	0.01786	2.15	0.01578
2.20	0.01390	2.25	0.01222	2.30	0.01072	2.35	0.009387
2.40	0.008198	2.45	0.007143	2.50	0.006210	2.55	0.005386
2.60	0.004661	2.65	0.004025	2.70	0.003467	2.75	0.002980
2.80	0.002555	2.85	0.002186	2.90	0.001866	2.95	0.001589
3.00	**0.001350**	3.05	0.001144	3.10	0.0009677	3.15	0.0008164
3.20	0.0006872	3.25	0.0005771	3.30	0.0004835	3.35	0.0004041
3.40	0.0003370	3.45	0.0002803	3.50	0.0002327	3.55	0.0001927
3.60	0.0001591	3.65	0.0001312	3.70	0.0001078	3.75	0.00008844
3.80	0.00007237	3.85	0.00005908	3.90	0.00004812	3.95	0.00003909
4.00	0.00003169	4.05	0.00002562	4.10	0.00002067	4.15	0.00001663
4.20	0.00001335	4.25	0.00001070	4.30	0.00000855	4.35	0.00000681
4.40	0.00000542	4.45	0.00000430	4.50	0.00000340	4.55	0.00000268
4.60	0.00000211	4.65	0.00000166	4.70	0.00000130	4.75	0.00000102
4.80	0.00000079	4.85	0.00000062	4.90	0.00000048	4.95	0.00000037

FIGURE 16-7

Normal Distribution, +1 Sigma

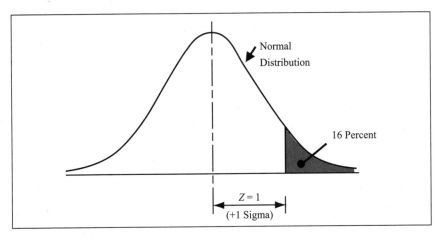

FIGURE 16-8

Normal Distribution, ±1 Sigma

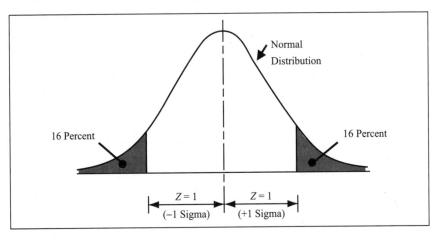

Problem 2

What is the probability of finding a shaft not greater than 1.002 inch?

We first must realize that 1.002 inch is 2 sigma above nominal (since sigma = 0.001 inch), so $Z = 2$. Using the Standardized

Normal Distribution Table in Figure 16–6 to get the probability, looking at $Z = 2$, we see that $P = 0.02275$.

Looking at the normal distribution curve at the top of the table (Figure 16–6), we can see that this P is the probability of being *greater than* 1.002 inches. Since we want *not greater than* 1.002 inches, we must subtract 0.02275 from 1.0000. Again, we know to do this because the total area under the curve, which represents all probabilities, equals 1. So, $1 - 0.02275 = 0.97725$.

Answer

$$P = 0.97725, \text{ or } 97.725 \text{ percent}$$

TIP

Assuming Normal Distribution

Use plotted data to check visually whether the data are normally distributed. When in doubt, plot more data. Unless the data are *dramatically* nonsymmetrical (data extremely off to one side) or *dramatically* bimodal (two lobes), assume a normal distribution. The data must *clearly* show a different distribution; if they do not, we assume the distribution is normal. Some computer programs use mathematical formulas to test whether data are normal, but optical inspection of the plotted data is generally sufficient. As you will see later, having a normal distribution allows you to directly use the absolute probability values in the Standardized Normal Distribution Table. However, if the distributions are *not* normal, the table values can still be used for comparison purposes.

As you will see in Chapter 19, most of the work we do in Six Sigma does not require a perfectly normal distribution because we are generally looking for relative change, not an absolute number based on the normal distribution table.

TIP

Normal Distribution Symmetry

Remembering that each half of the normal distribution curve is a mirror image of the other, we can use data given for the plus side to solve problems related to both sides.

Problem 3

In the shaft process previously discussed, what is the probability of getting a shaft below 0.9978 inch in diameter?

This shaft diameter is 0.0022 inch below nominal (1 – 0.9978 inch). Since sigma = 0.0010 inch, this is 2.2 sigma below nominal, so $Z = 2.2$. Looking at the Standardized Normal Distribution Table (Figure 16–6), $Z = 2.2$, and we see that $P = 0.0139$. Therefore, 1.39 percent of the data points would occur above a positive 2.2 sigma. Since the negative side of the probability table is a mirror image of the positive side, the probability also applies to a negative 2.2 sigma.

Answer

$$P = 0.0139, \text{ or } 1.39 \text{ percent}$$

TIP

No values occur exactly at a Z point.

In using a standardized normal distribution curve, all values are assumed to be above or below a Z point. For example, if you wanted to know what percent of values are above $Z = 2$, it would be the same as the percent of values at or above $Z = 2$.

For simplicity, the previous shaft data had a sigma of 0.0010 inch. We used this value to make calculations and understanding easier. Usually the sigma doesn't correlate with the bin edges, nor is it such an even number. This in no way changes the logic or diminishes the value of the Standardized Normal Distribution Table (Figure 16–6), as shown in the following problems.

Problem 4

Using the shaft example, let's assume that the customer has complained that the amount of variation in the shafts is causing him process problems. The customer is especially critical of shafts less than 0.9980 inch and greater than 1.0020 inches (more than 0.0020 inch from nominal).

In response, the lathe is overhauled. On taking another 1,000 measurements after the overhaul, it is determined that the average has stayed at 1.0000 inch, but the sigma has been reduced from 0.0010 to 0.0007 inch.

The reduced sigma means that the variation between shafts is less than it was before the overhaul. We want to communicate to the customer what improvement he can expect in future shipments—specifically what reduction he will see in shafts more than 0.0020 inch above or below the nominal 1.0000-inch diameter.

Before the overhaul (Problem 1, sigma = 0.0010 inch), we found that the probability of finding a shaft at least 0.0020 inch above 1.0000 inch in diameter was 0.02275. Given that both sides of the curve are mirror images, we double that number to calculate the chances of being at least 0.0020 inch ± nominal:

$$P = 0.02275 \times 2 = 0.0455, \text{ or } 4.55 \text{ percent} \qquad (P \text{ before the overhaul})$$

We must now calculate the P with the new reduced sigma (0.0007 inch). First, we see how many sigma "fit" between nominal and 0.0020 inch. We use the plus side first because that is the data given to us in the Standardized Normal Distribution Table (Figure 16–6).

We see that 0.0020 inch/0.0007 inch = 2.86 sigma fit! This gives us the Z to use in the Standardized Normal Distribution Table (Figure 16–6).

Using the Standardized Normal Distribution Table (Figure 16–6), looking at Z = 2.85 (the closest table data point), the P value we read from the table is 0.002186. So, 0.2186 percent of the shafts will be at least 0.0020 inch above nominal. We double this to include those at least 0.0020 inch below 1.0000-inch diameter:

$$2 \times 0.002186 = 0.004372$$

The total P is 0.004372, or 0.4372 percent (P after the overhaul).

Answer

Since the process had been making 4.55 percent at 0.0020 inch above or below 1.0000 inch and it is now making 0.4372 percent, the customer can expect to see 9.6 percent (0.437/4.55) of their former problem shafts.

Problem 5

Let's change the above problem again to make it even more realistic. After the overhaul, the lathe sigma is reduced to 0.0007 inch (same as above), but the average shaft diameter is now 1.0005 inches. The process plot is still normal. Will the customer be receiving fewer problem shafts than before the overhaul?

Since the process average is no longer centered at the 1.0000-inch nominal, the amount of product outside the 0.9980- to 1.0020-inch target is different for the large diameters than for the small diameters, so calculate each independently.

First, we will calculate the P for the too-large shafts. As before, we see how many sigma (0.0007 inch) fit between the new process average (1.0005 inch) and the +1.0020-inch upper limit:

$$\frac{1.0020 \text{ inches} - 1.0005 \text{ inches}}{0.0007 \text{ inch}} = 2.143 \text{ sigma fit}$$

Looking at the Standardized Normal Distribution Table (Figure 16–6), we see that the P at a Z of 2.15 (closest value to 2.143) is 0.01578. That means that 1.578 percent of the shafts will be 1.0020 inches in diameter or larger.

Looking at the too-small shafts, we perform a similar calculation. First, find the value for the difference between the process average and the lower end of the target (the process average is 1.0005 inches and the lower target value is 0.9980 inch). The difference is 1.0005 inches – 0.9980 inch = 0.0025 inch.

We then see how many sigma (0.0007 inch) fit: 0.0025 inch/0.0007 inch = 3.57 sigma. Although we must use the data on the positive end of the curve, we know that the mirror image would be identical. Looking at the P value for a Z of 3.55, we get $P = 0.0001927$. So 0.019 percent of the shafts will be 0.9980 inch or smaller.

Answer

When we add the too-large- and too-small-diameter shafts, we get 1.578 percent + 0.019 percent = 1.60 percent of the shafts will be at least 0.0020 inch off the 1.0000-inch nominal. This 1.60 percent is less than the 4.45 percent the customer was receiving before the overhaul, so the customer will be receiving a better product.

Note, however, that 1.60 percent is much higher than the 0.4372 percent (Problem 4) the customer would receive if the process were centered.

This change in both the average and the sigma is not unusual in a process change. However, it is usually not difficult to get the process mean back to the target center (in this case, 1.0000-inch diameter). If the process center is put back to nominal, we get the 10-fold improvement we saw in the earlier problem.

TIP

Adjusting the Mean of a Process Versus Reducing Its Sigma

Normally moving the mean of a process is easier than trying to reduce its sigma.

Changing mean is often accomplished just by choosing the center around which the process will be run; it requires no major process change. A sigma reduction often requires a significant change in the process itself, like dramatically slowing the process or changing the equipment being used.

Note that in the above cases, the Standardized Normal Distribution Table (Figure 16–6) Z values that were used were those closest to the calculated values of Z. There was no attempt to extrapolate or to go to another table or computer program for greater accuracy. Either would have been possible, but if you look at the relative values obtained versus the changes being noted, the greater accuracy was not required. Often the calculation accuracy far exceeds the requirements of the output results.

TIP

Using *Excel* to Get Normal Distribution Values

Those wishing to use the computer to get the probability values for various values of Z can use *Excel*. After bringing up the *Excel* worksheet, click on the Paste or the Insert function in the toolbar. Under Category, click on Statistical. Then, under Function, click on NORMSDIST. When you enter a Z value, it gives you the probability values using the left end of the distribution as the reference zero, whereas the Standardized Normal Distribution Table (Figure 16–6) uses the right end of the distribution as zero. To convert either one to the other, simply subtract the value from 1.

For example, if you enter $Z = 2$ in the *Excel* NORMSDIST, you get a probability value of 0.97725. This is the probability of being less than the Z value. Thus, $1.00000 - 0.97725 = 0.02275$ is the probability of being greater than Z, which matches the probability given for $Z = 2$ on the Standardized Normal Distribution Table (Figure 16–6).

Just for information purposes, the 6 sigma process is some-times referred to as "3 defects per million." If you look at the Standardized Normal Distribution Table (Figure 16–6), you will see that 3 defects per million is 4.5 sigma, not 6 sigma. The 6 sigma short-term target is tighter than the 4.5 sigma long-term goal because it assumes Motorola's 1.5 sigma process drift will take place over time, and allowance is made for this expected drift. The idea was that if you started with a process that was 6 sigma short-term, you would have a 4.5 sigma process when the expected long-term drift was included, which would generate 3 defects per million products.

PLOTTING DATA

There are hundreds of computer programs available that will plot data and do some degree of statistical analysis. Some of these are quite good; many are somewhat confusing. Generally the more ambitious the program (three-dimensional plots in various colors, every type of plot imaginable, esoteric statistical analysis), the more chances of getting an output that doesn't tell the desired story. This problem stems from incomplete or confus-ing directions or help screens, the user's not taking the time to understand the details of the program, or even errors within the program.

Case Study: Blindly Using a Plotting Program

In a review of Six Sigma projects, the presenter was displaying what he described as "normal" data consisting of 100 individual data points, with the ±3 sigma lines as shown on the graph in Figure 16–9.

At the end of the presentation, one person asked how approximately 20 percent of the data points could be beyond the 3 sigma limits since the limits were supposedly calculated from the data points displayed and 99.7 percent of the data points in a normal distribution are supposed to be within the ±3 sigma limits. This was an important question since the plotting program used was the designated statistical program for the whole corporation.

Only later did someone discover that within the program was a default that used the last 10 data points entered to calculate the 3 sigma limits.

FIGURE 16–9

Plot of Normal Data Consisting of 100 Individual Data Points
Based on 100 Process Samples

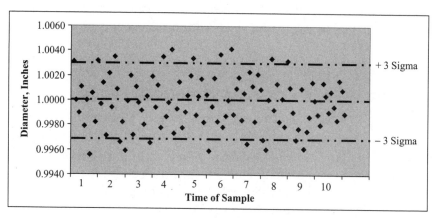

This case study is problematic for several reasons. First, other than the questioner, no one else demonstrated a basic understanding of what the 3 sigma limits meant; no one else tested the graph for reasonableness. Second, it's troublesome that the default in the computer program would use only the last 10 points entered to calculate the 3 sigma limits (you will learn later that a *minimum* of 11 points is needed to get a decent estimate of sigma, with 30 points preferred). Third, almost no one using this program had bothered to understand how the program worked (or its defaults) or the basis of its output. Fourth, what caused the last group of data to be so different?

Many programs are so forbidding that the user is just relieved to get an output. There is also a belief that any graph output is some verification that the input is correct and that the output is meaningful. Many of these programs are powerful, but they require care to use.

Any users of a statistical program not completely familiar to them should do some manual work with the data before using the program. They should then input a very simplified set of data where they already know the outcome. Finally, the output should be carefully tested for reasonableness.

In this book we will use *Excel* to generate our graphs. This is *not* because *Excel* is the best program for graphs (it isn't) but because I'm assuming that most users of this text have Microsoft's *Excel* on their computers. Details on the use of other graphing programs can be found in the user's manual accompanying those other programs.

USING THE *EXCEL* GRAPHING PROGRAM

I will go into more detail than you probably need in case you are less *Excel* oriented. If you are completely familiar with graphing with *Excel*, you can quickly glance over this section.

First, make sure *Excel*'s *Data Analysis* program is loaded into Tools on your computer. Bring up Microsoft *Excel*. On the header on the top of the screen, go to Tools. See if Data Analysis is one of the options available. If not, under Tools go to Add-ins. Check the boxes opposite Analysis ToolPak and Analysis ToolPak VBA, then OK. If it is not available, you will have to insert the Microsoft *Office Professional* disk and install it. You may have to close *Excel* then reopen it to see Data Analysis as one of the options. For now, go back out of Tools.

Copy the following 50 numbers into an *Excel* worksheet, column A.

1.0004	0.9996	0.9991	1.0008
1.0001	1.0005	0.9995	1
1.0012	0.9996	0.9998	0.9997
0.9986	0.9985	0.9999	0.9991
1	1.0004	0.9996	0.9993
1.0002	1.0006	0.9988	0.9991
1.0009	1.0002	0.9994	1.0014
0.9978	1.0013	0.9982	0.9984
1.0015	0.9996	1.001	1.0009
1.0016	0.9998	0.999	0.9998
0.9989	0.9989	1.0001	0.9993
0.9972	1.0003	1.0009	1.0019
1.0024	0.9996		

These numbers represent 50 shaft diameter readings we may expect from the previously discussed shaft process. After copying these numbers, highlight and then Order these numbers using the AZ down-arrow option in the second row header at the top of the screen. (If this option doesn't show, go into Data on the toolbar and you will see the AZ down arrow opposite Sort. Click on Ascending.) After ordering these, the top number will be 0.9972 and the bottom number will be 1.0024.

In column B, row 1, enter the formula = (bottom or maximum number) − (top or minimum number), which in this case will be = A50 − A1. This will give the difference between the largest and smallest shaft diameter, which will be 0.0052.

In that same column B, second row, insert the formula = 1.02*B1/7. This gives us bin sizes for 7 bins. (See the following Tip for calculating the number of bins.) The 1.02 makes the total bin widths slightly wider than the data range. If we have more data, we can use more bins by changing the denominator from 7 to the higher bin quantity. With 7 bins, the bin width shown in B2 will be 0.0007577.

Now we have to show the specific bin edges. In C1, insert the formula = A1 − 0.01*B1. In this example it will put a value of 0.99715 in C1. This gives the left bin edge, which is slightly less than the minimum data value. Then, in C2 insert the formula = C1 + B2. This determines that the next bin edge will be the number in C1 plus the bin width. C2 in this example will then be 0.99791. The $'s in this case "freeze" the bin width B2 for use in the next steps.

Under Edit, copy C2. Highlight C3 through C8 (you would highlight more if you had more bins.) Then click Edit, Paste Special, and Formulas. This gives you the edge values for each of the remaining bins. In this example C8 should show bin value 1.00245, the right edge of the last bin. This value is slightly higher than the maximum data number.

Now, go to Tools in the top header, and click Data Analysis, and then Histogram. When this screen comes up, highlight column A (your data) and enter it as the Input Range. Then click on the second box (Bin Range) and enter the highlighted bin ranges from column C. The options New Worksheet Ply and Chart Output should be chosen, then click OK. The histogram will come up. Drag down the right bottom corner to extend the vertical axis. The histogram should look similar to the one in Figure 16–10.

FIGURE 16–10

Excel Histogram

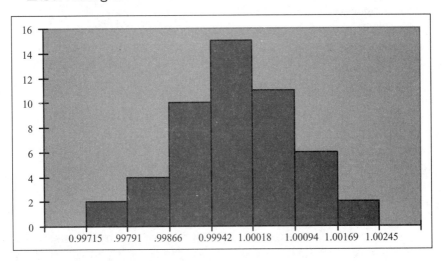

The bottom horizontal x axis, as labeled in *Excel*, makes it look like the bin values are in the middle of the bins rather than on the right edges. This was modified for the above illustration. Also, if you get more (or fewer) label digits than shown above, you can modify them to match the above (or whatever you desire) by formatting the bin-edge column in the *Excel* spreadsheet. You may want to add definition to the wording on the axis. However, in this book we are more interested in the histogram shape than the labels.

TIP
Rule of Thumb for Choosing the Number of Bins to Use in a Histogram

$$\text{No. of bins} = \sqrt{\text{No. of data points}}$$

Note: This is only a general guideline. Feel free to experiment.

CHAPTER 16 REVIEW

1. Plotting data is a step needed in implementing many of the Six Sigma tools.

2. Data needed for histograms and Standardized Normal Distribution Table analysis are often readily available.

3. Using histograms to compare supposedly similar areas or year-to-year performance helps to reveal unexpected differences and areas of opportunity. Using the Standardized Normal Distribution Table (Figure 16–6) to evaluate data on a normal distribution or to compare two processes with similarly shaped histograms can often help to quantify a problem.

4. *Excel* can be used to make histograms or get normal distribution values.

5. A graphing program may be powerful, but the user needs to fully understand it.

6. You can perform real Six Sigma work by using histograms and the normal distribution table.

Testing for Statistical Differences in Data

Qui rogat, non errat.   (Who asks isn't wrong.)

—Latin saying

Part Five, which includes Chapters 17 through 19, gives formulas for determining minimum sample sizes. These formulas are to be used when checking for statistical significance on both variables and proportional data.

Also included in Part Five are the statistical tests to determine if a change in data is large enough to be statistically significant at a 95 percent confidence level.

Chapter 19 explains why we can often use data based on a normal distribution to analyze problems that have nonnormal distributions.

CHAPTER 17

Testing for Statistically Significant Change Using Variables Data

What you will learn in this chapter is to use limited samples of variables data to make judgments on whether a population or process has changed. We will be comparing samples to the population and samples to each other.

Why do we have to check for statistical significance when comparing two sets of data? Why don't we just take the average and standard deviation of both sets of sample data and then make a judgment on whether the populations represented by those samples are different?

To answer those questions, let's look at the following two groups of data showing the price/earnings ratios on stocks:

Two Sets of Data on Stock Price/Earnings Ratios

	Group 1	Group 2
	20.3	18.8
	19.5	17.7
	23.8	23.4
	16.9	22.9
	20.1	22.0
	27.4	19.8
	22.4	18.5
	25.3	24.0
	18.7	24.8
	23.5	17.5
	27.3	15.5
	21.0	21.2
	18.0	26.8
	24.8	25.1
	23.6	18.3
Average	22.173	21.087
Standard deviation	3.278	3.353

Group 1 sample data certainly has a higher average and a lower standard deviation, so why can't we just say that the population of stocks from which Group 1 was taken has a higher price/earnings ratio and less variation (standard deviation) compared to the population of Group 2?

The reason we *can't* do this is that there is some "luck of the draw" related to sample data, and the sample never exactly represents the population from which it is drawn. For example, if we take two different samples from the same population and compare the two samples, one sample will often have a different average and standard deviation compared to the other sample. The determination we must make is if a difference between two samples is great enough to be statistically significant. Only then can we say whether the populations from which they are drawn are likely to be different. At the end of this chapter, after we have learned the appropriate formulas, we will take a second look at these two sets of data and see if they are truly significantly different.

Before checking for significant differences between groups of data, we first want to determine the minimum sample size required. This is important because taking a sample that is too small can cause invalid estimates, but taking excessive samples is costly.

The formulas in this chapter are used for the Define, Measure, Analysis, Improve, and Control steps in the DMAIC process.

In Chapter 15 on probability, we learned to judge whether an event was due to random or assignable cause. In all cases we knew the odds of the random event, like 0.5 on a coin flip or ⅙ on rolling a die. An event that was nonrandom hinted at a problem or an opportunity.

In Chapter 16 on data plots and distributions, we plotted a large quantity of data from a sample or population to see trends or changes. We would use the plot to see the data distribution. We used a standardized normal distribution table to perform further analysis. As in the probability chapter, once we had an identified distribution, we used this knowledge to judge whether an event was due to a random or assignable cause.

Similarly, in this chapter we conduct statistical tests on variables data to determine if a change is large enough to be significant at a 95 percent confidence level.

Changes in Real Processes, Variables Data

Manufacturing
Compare dimensional samples from two similar production lines, or compare shift samples on one line to look for significant differences.

Sales
Compare samples from different salespeople on sales dollars generated using samples from many random days.

Marketing
Compare samples of advertising dollars spent in a city over a period of time versus the sales generated in that city to see if advertising dollars makes a significant difference in sales.

Accounting and Software Development
Sample error rates and look for differences among people doing similar work, using samples from many individual days.

Receivables
Check for correlations between sample delinquent receivables and Dun & Bradstreet (D&B) rating. Use data from many individual days.

Insurance
Sample costs among different treatment centers on similar procedures, using data from many individual days.

DEFINITION

variables data Variables data are measurable and generally in decimal form. Theoretically you could look at enough decimal places to find that no two values are exactly the same. *Continuous data* is another term used for this type of data. The resolution of variables data measurements should be such that at least 10 possible data "steps" are within the tolerance or area of interest.

TIP
Sample Size Rule of Thumb on Variables Data

To calculate sigma on variables data, a rule-of-thumb minimum sample size n of 11 is needed, with a preferable sample size n of 30 or more.

To calculate an average, the sample size n can be as low as 6. However, since we normally must calculate sigma at the same time, the minimum n of 11 and preferable n of 30 is the standard.

This rule of thumb should be used only when it is not possible to calculate a specific minimum sample size. This situation would exist where we did not know the population sigma or were not sure of the accuracy we needed.

Case Study: Obscene Scrap Call

In a process that ran 24 hours per day, an inspector took product readings continuously. Every time 7 pieces were measured, a computer program calculated an average and sigma from these 7 pieces. Using that average and sigma, the computer projected the percentage of product that was outside specifications. The results of these calculations were then displayed in the operator's booth, which was at the other end of the manufacturing plant. If the projected percentage of the product that was outside specifications was too high, the product was put into "scrap," and it remained there until the calculations on another 7-piece sample showed an acceptable defect projection.

The scrap decision was communicated back to the machine operator, who was supposed to make adjustments to bring the product quality back to acceptable levels. The operator had learned from experience, however, that these scrap decisions were sometimes invalid and that the scrap would often cancel out on the next sample without any process adjustments being made. Therefore, the operator would delay adjusting the process until several scrap calls occurred in a row.

The result was that scrap time was excessive, bad product was shipped (the erroneous scrap calls also missed some bad product), and the plant production people had no faith in the quality system. The machine operators had even coined an obscene phrase for the basis of the scrap decision. The first half of this phrase was "sigma," which I am not sure they fully understood. But they certainly knew what the last half of the coined phrase meant!

As it was stated in the earlier tip on sample size, the rule of thumb for the minimum sample size for a valid sigma estimate is 11. The quality system in this example was using a sample size of 7! The quality manager was very hesitant to increase the sample size because he thought the system reaction time would then be too slow. It took much convincing for him to even try a larger sample size.

However, when the sample size was eventually increased to 15, the erroneous scrap calls were substantially reduced (this was verified by data taken before and after the change), the outgoing quality was improved, scrap time was reduced, and faith in the quality system was restored. The reaction time of the system never became an issue because having valid scrap calls was far more important. The scrap time reduction alone was worth over $100,000 per year, and there was a negligible cost for implementation.

Almost any formal or informal quality system has a sample size that is used to make decisions. Even where there are no formal rules, someone makes a judgment on how many items should be reviewed before making a determination. This is true in reviewing office staff output, incoming product, medical errors, accounting errors, programming mistakes, and so on. If too many examples are required, a decision is delayed and poor performance is missed. If judgment is made on too small of a sample, then erroneous calls are often made.

> ### Labeling Averages and Standard Deviations
>
> If we want to label the average of a population, we use $\overline{X}$; if we want to label the sample averages, we use $\overline{x}$.
>
> Similarly, we label the standard deviation (sigma) of a population S and the sample standard deviations s.
>
> We will use $\overline{X}$, S, $\overline{x}$, and s in this book rather than the Greek letters used in some books. Both forms are in use widely and acceptable.
>
> ### Population Versus Sample
>
> We seldom have *all* the data on a population, so we make an estimate about the population based on large or multiple samples.

ESTIMATING A POPULATION AVERAGE $\overline{X}$ AND SIGMA S

> ### TIP
>
> Maximize the sample size to estimate the population average and sigma.
>
> The greater the sample size n ("n is your friend"), the better your estimate of the population average and standard deviation.

Here are two methods of determining the population $\overline{X}$ and S, the first from a large sample and the second from multiple samples of similar size n.

> ### Method 1. Estimating the Population $\overline{X}$ and S from a Large Sample
>
> You can estimate a population average $\overline{X}$ and sigma S from the $\overline{x}$ and s of a large sample that has a minimum sample size of $n = 30$. Assume that the population average and sigma are the same as those of the large sample.

You can use the second method to estimate the population sigma S if you have two or more samples of similar size n.

The formula is shown in the following box:

Method 2. Estimating the Population $\overline{X}$ and S from Multiple Samples of Similar Size n

$$\overline{X} = \frac{\overline{x}_1 + \overline{x}_2}{2}$$

$\overline{X}$ = population average
$\overline{x}_1$ = average from sample 1
$\overline{x}_2$ = average from sample 2

$$S = \sqrt{\frac{s_1^2 + s_2^2}{2}}$$

S = population sigma
s_1 = sigma of sample 1
s_2 = sigma of sample 2

If you have three or more samples, modify the formulas accordingly, by putting more sample sigmas or averages in the numerator and dividing by the total number of samples.

For example, let's say you have $s_1 = 16$ and $s_2 = 12$. Then

$$S = \sqrt{\frac{s_1^2 + s_2^2}{2}} = \sqrt{\frac{16^2 + 12^2}{2}} = 14.14$$

If the sample sizes are substantially different, use the s from the largest sample for the estimate of S because the confidence related to a small sample is suspect. You can also use a computer program that will compensate for different sample sizes, but this is not normally necessary.

Problem 1

You have data from two samples taken from a stable process, with no other knowledge of the process population:

Sample 1	Sample 2
$n = 15$	$n = 42$
$\overline{x} = 15.05$	$\overline{x} = 15.38$
$s = 1.58$	$s = 1.46$

What is the estimate for the population average and $\overline{X}$ sigma S?

Since the sample sizes n are quite different from each other, use the larger sample. Also, since the size of sample 2 is over 30, we feel comfortable that it is a reasonable estimate. So the estimate for the population is the following:

$$\overline{X} = 15.38$$
$$S = 1.46$$

Problem 2
You have data from three samples taken from a stable process, with no other knowledge of the process population:

Sample 1	Sample 2	Sample 3
$n = 16$	$n = 18$	$n = 15$
$\overline{x}_1 = 14.96$	$\overline{x}_2 = 15.05$	$\overline{x}_3 = 15.04$
$s_1 = 1.52$	$s_2 = 1.49$	$s_3 = 1.53$

What is the estimate for the population average $\overline{X}$ and sigma S?

Since all three samples have a similar sample size n, we will use the above formulas to calculate our estimate for the population.

$$\overline{X} = \frac{\overline{x}_1 + \overline{x}_2 + \overline{x}_3}{3}$$

$$= \frac{14.96 + 15.05 + 15.04}{3} = 15.017$$

$$S = \sqrt{\frac{s_1^2 + s_2^2 + s_3^2}{3}}$$

$$= \sqrt{\frac{1.52^2 + 1.49^2 + 1.53^2}{3}}$$

$$= \sqrt{\frac{6.8714}{3}} = 1.513$$

FORMULA
Calculating Minimum Sample Size and Sensitivity, Variables Data

To calculate minimum sample size on variables data, use the formula below:

$$n = \left(\frac{Z*S}{h}\right)^2$$

n = minimum sample size on variables data   (Always round up.)
Z = confidence level   (When in doubt, use $Z = 1.96$, as in the following Tip.)
S = population standard deviation
h = smallest change we want to be able to sense   (When in doubt, use
      h = total tolerance/10, or $h = 0.6S$.)

Note that the formula shown above can be rewritten as:

$$h = \sqrt{\frac{Z^2 * S^2}{n}}$$

This allows us to calculate what sensitivity h (change) we can sense with a given sample size and confidence level.

A lot of judgment goes into calculating sample size. Often the final sample size will be a compromise between cost (both product and inspection) and customer need. The formulas allow you to make sample size a knowledge-based decision rather than just a guess.

Looking at the components of the sample size formula, we see that the sample size n is not only influenced by the sensitivity (h) required but also by the process sigma. Sometimes this formula will point out that the sample size requirement is so excessive that only a process improvement (reduced sigma) or a loosening of the customer's requirements (increased h) will make sampling viable.

TIP
Z, Confidence of Results

Z relates to the probability, or confidence, we are looking for. For one-tailed questions (like greater-than), use $Z = 1.64$ for 95 percent confidence. On two-tailed problems (like greater-than *or* less-than), use $Z = 1.96$ for 95 percent confidence.

We normally test to a 95 percent confidence.

Assume a problem is two-tailed unless it has been described specifically as one-tailed. *So the Z will normally be 1.96.*

The alternatives to sampling include automatic inspection or 100 percent process sorting. This use of the sample size formulas to understand these options is a very productive use of the Six Sigma process.

You can find countless tables and computer programs that will test significance at many different confidence levels. If you look at a low enough confidence level, you may find differences that are significant that were *not* significant at a 95 percent confidence level. But at lower confidence levels, you are increasing the chance of erroneous conclusions. Also, using higher confidence levels buys you little since you usually have to rerun any test to see if the results replicate. If you recall from Chapter 15 on probability, running two tests at a 0.95 probability minimizes "chance" to $p = 0.05 \times 0.05 = 0.0025$. There is normally no reason to test to a higher confidence than 95 percent since you may miss real opportunity.

Problem 3

Administrators at a high school had just gotten the results from a national achievement test, and they wanted to know how many random results they would have to review before deciding, with 95 percent confidence, if the performance of the students had *changed*. The historical sigma on this test was 1.24.

The administrators wanted to be able to sense a change of 0.6S, which is 0.744:

$$n = \left(\frac{Z * S}{h} \right)^2$$

$$= \left(\frac{1.96 * 1.24}{0.744} \right)^2$$

$$= 10.67$$

So they would have to look at the results from at least 11 tests to see if the performance had changed 0.744, with a 95 percent confidence.

Problem 4

Administrators at a high school had just gotten the results from a national achievement test, and they wanted to know how many random results they would have to review before deciding, with 95 percent confidence, if the performance of the students had *improved*. The historical sigma on this test was 1.24.

The administrators wanted to be able to sense an improvement of 0.6S, which is 0.744. Note that this problem is now one-tailed because the administrators want to see only if the students improved. This changes the value of Z to 1.64:

$$n = \left(\frac{Z * S}{h} \right)^2$$

$$= \left(\frac{1.64 * 1.24}{0.744} \right)^2$$

$$= 7.47$$

So they would have to look at the results from at least 8 tests to see if the performance had improved 0.744, with a 95 percent confidence.

Note that by only looking for improved scores, the minimum sample size is reduced from 11 to 8. However, knowing if change occurred only on the up side is usually not sufficient because the school would at some point be concerned about change on both the up and down sides. Because of this, the sample size is usually determined by a two-tailed $Z = 1.96$, as in Problem 3, giving a minimum sample size of 11.

Problem 5
Before doing the calculations in Problems 3 and 4, someone had already tabulated the results from 20 tests. At 95 perent confidence, what change in results (h) could be sensed from reviewing this many results versus the minimum 0.744 change target?

The historical sigma on this test was 1.24:

$$h = \sqrt{\frac{Z^2 * S^2}{n}}$$

$$= \sqrt{\frac{1.96^2 * 1.24^2}{20}}$$

$$= 0.543$$

So the sensitivity on 20 results is 0.543 versus the 0.744 target. The school would be able to sense a smaller change. This shows the benefit of a larger sample size of $n = 20$ versus $n = 11$.

USING A SAMPLE TO CHECK FOR A CHANGE VERSUS A POPULATION

We will use a three-step process:

1. First check the distributions to see if the data histogram shapes (population versus sample) are substantially different.
2. If the distribution shapes are not substantially different, then see if the sigmas are significantly different.
3. If neither of the above tests shows a difference, we then check if the averages are significantly different.

If we sense a significant difference at any point in the above steps, we stop and try to find the cause. Any significant difference is potentially important since it can affect costs, quality, and so on.

TIP

Don't use data analysis alone to drive decisions.

The following formulas will give you the ability to detect change. The reaction to any analytical finding should be tempered by common sense and expert knowledge. This should not stop you from pursuing a finding that violates common sense or expert knowledge because it is not uncommon to discover that some preconceived notions are invalid. However, tread softly because the analysis could also be wrong.

Remember, we are testing to a 95 percent confidence level, which means that 5 percent of the time you could be wrong. And the 5 percent is optimistic! That is the mathematical error. You also have gauge error, sampling error, and other types of error in addition to the 5 percent error. Probably 10 percent is a more realistic estimate of *actual* possible error.

That is why an additional test under controlled conditions is always needed to validate a finding.

1. Checking the Distributions

First, it may be necessary to plot a large number of individual measurements to verify that the sample distribution shape is similar to that of the earlier population. Although a process distribution will normally be similar over time, it is important to verify this, especially when running a test or after a policy change, machine wreck, personnel change, and so on. We are only concerned with gross differences, like one plot being very strongly skewed or bimodal versus the other. If plotting is required, it will need a sample size of at least 36. If there is a substantial change in the distribution shape, there is no reason to do further tests because we know the process has changed and we should be trying to understand the change cause and ramifications.

If there are outliers (data values clearly separate from the general distribution), you must determine the causes of those data points before you perform any quantitative statistical analysis on the data. If you can confidently determine that the questionable data points are due to an error in collecting or entering data and they don't reflect the process, then you can remove the data points. If the wild data points are *not* an input error, then you have found a potential problem that must be resolved.

TIP
Examining Plotted Data

Visually examining plotted data will often give insights that can't be seen with any quantitative method.

Here is an example showing why you can't just look at the numerical statistics, and why you first have to examine the plotted data. Below are two sets of 50 pieces of data, with the averages and standard deviations shown below each set of data. Notice that the averages and standard deviations of both groups of data are basically the same.

Data Set 1

0.9991	0.9991	0.9998	1.0009
0.9978	0.9993	1.0002	1.0009
0.9982	0.9993	1.0002	1.001
0.9984	0.9994	1.0003	1.001
0.9985	0.9995	1.0003	1.0012
0.9986	0.9996	1.0003	1.0013
0.9988	0.9996	1.0004	1.0014
0.9989	0.9996	1.0004	1.0015
0.9989	0.9996	1.0005	1.0015
0.999	0.9996	1.0006	1.0015
0.999	0.9998	1.0006	1.0016
0.9991	0.9998	1.0008	
0.9972	0.9998	1.0009	

Average = 0.999892
Standard deviation = 0.00105

Data Set 2

0.9992	0.9993	1.0000	0.9995
0.9992	0.9993	0.9995	1.0000
0.9992	0.9993	0.9995	1.0000
0.9992	0.9993	0.9996	1.0000
0.9993	0.9993	1.0000	1.0000
0.9993	0.9994	1.0000	1.0002
1.0000	0.9994	0.9993	1.0034
0.9993	0.9994	1.0000	1.0025
0.9993	0.9994	1.0000	1.003
0.9993	1.0000	0.9994	1.0032
0.9993	0.9994	1.0000	1.0021
0.9993	0.9994	1.0000	
0.9993	0.9995	1.0000	

Average = 0.999896
Standard deviation = 0.00105

Now we want to look at the data plots, shown in Figures 17–1 and 17–2, for both sets of data. Note that the data distributions

FIGURE 17–1

Plot of Data Set 1

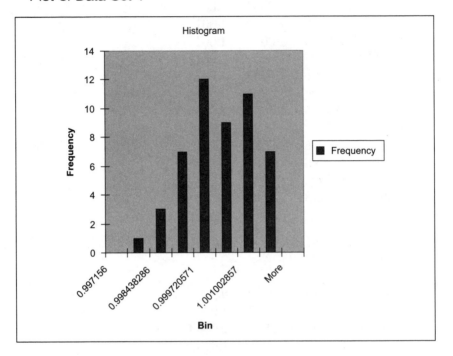

FIGURE 17–2

Plot of Data Set 2

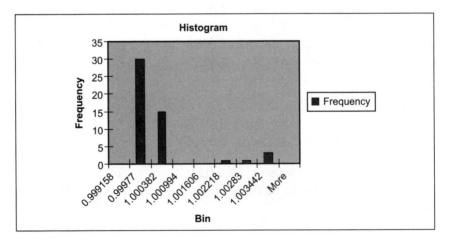

have completely different shapes. The distributions don't just have a wider spread, nor did their centers just change. They have a totally different shape.

These processes cannot be compared using standard numerical tests because they are two completely different processes. They might have been the same processes at some time in the past—at least you thought they were, otherwise you probably wouldn't be comparing them now. However, due to a machine wreck or an unknown process change, they are no longer similar. Trying to compare them now is like comparing apples to oranges. This difference cannot be seen by just looking at the data averages and standard deviations; plotting is required.

Note that discovering this difference is usually a good thing because it often gives insight to some process deviation or change that was unknown and should be addressed.

2. Checking the Sigmas

If the process distribution has not changed qualitatively (looking at the data plots) then you can do some quantitative tests. The first thing to check is if the sigma has changed significantly. The sigma on a process does not normally change unless a basic change in the process has occurred. To see if the sigma has changed, we calculate a *chi-square test value* (chi$_t^2$).

FORMULA

Chi-Square Test of a Sample Sigma *s* Versus a Population Sigma *S*

$$\text{Chi}_t^2 = \frac{(n-1)\,s^2}{S^2}$$

n = sample size
s = sample sigma
S = population sigma

We compare the calculated chi$_t^2$ results to the values in the Simplified Chi-Square Distribution Table provided in Figure 17–3. If the chi$_t^2$ test value we calculated is less than the table low value or greater than the table high value, we are 95 percent confident that the sample sigma *s* is different from the sigma *S* of the population.

FIGURE 17–3

Simplified Chi-Square Distribution Table
To Test a Sample Sigma s (with Sample Size n) Versus
a Population Sigma S

	95% Confident They Are Different If Chi$_t^2$ Is			95% Confident They Are Different If Chi$_t^2$ Is	
	< Low	Or > High		< Low	Or > High
n	Low Test	High Test	n	Low Test	High Test
6	0.831209	12.83249	36	20.56938	53.20331
7	1.237342	14.44935	37	21.33587	54.43726
8	1.689864	16.01277	38	22.10562	55.66798
9	2.179725	17.53454	39	22.87849	56.89549
10	2.700389	19.02278	40	23.6543	58.12005
11	3.246963	20.4832	41	24.43306	59.34168
12	3.815742	21.92002	42	25.21452	60.56055
13	4.403778	23.33666	43	25.99866	61.77672
14	5.008738	24.73558	44	26.78537	62.99031
15	5.628724	26.11893	45	27.57454	64.20141
16	6.262123	27.48836	46	28.36618	65.41013
17	6.907664	28.84532	47	29.16002	66.61647
18	7.564179	30.19098	48	29.95616	67.82064
19	8.230737	31.52641	49	30.7545	69.02257
20	8.906514	32.85234	50	31.55493	70.22236
21	9.590772	34.16958	55	35.58633	76.19206
22	10.28291	35.47886			
23	10.98233	36.78068	60	39.66185	82.11737
24	11.68853	38.07561			
25	12.40115	39.36406	65	43.77594	88.00398
26	13.11971	40.6465	70	47.92412	93.85648
27	13.84388	41.92314			
28	14.57337	43.19452	80	56.30887	105.4727
29	15.30785	44.46079			
30	16.04705	45.72228	90	64.79339	116.989
31	16.79076	46.97922	100	73.3611	128.4219
32	17.53872	48.23192			
33	18.29079	49.48044			
34	19.04666	50.7251			
35	19.80624	51.96602			

If there has been a significant change in the sigma, there is no reason to do further tests, and we should be trying to understand the change cause and ramifications.

3. Checking the Averages

If in steps 1 and 2 we have not found that either the distribution or sigma has changed significantly, we are then free to test whether the sample average is significantly different from the population average. We will have to calculate a *t-test value* (t_t) to compare to a value in the Simplified t Distribution Table in Figure 17–4.

FORMULA

t Test of a Population Average $\overline{X}$ Versus a Sample Average $\overline{x}$

$$t_t = \frac{|\overline{x} - \overline{X}|}{\frac{s}{\sqrt{n}}}$$

$\overline{X}$ = population average
$\overline{x}$ = sample average
s = sample sigma
n = sample size

$|\overline{x} - \overline{X}|$ is the absolute value of the difference of the averages, so ignore a minus sign in the difference.

We compare this calculated t-test (t_t) value against the value in the Simplified t Distribution Table in Figure 17–4. If our calculated t-test (t_t) value is greater than the value in the table, then we are 95 percent confident that the sample average is significantly different from the population average.

Problem 6

We have made a process change on our infamous lathe that is machining shafts. We want to know, with 95 percent confidence, if the "before" process, with an average $\overline{X}$ of 1.0003 inches and a sigma S of 0.00170 inch, has changed.

We use our three-step process to look for change. Assume that we first plotted some data from after the change and compared it with a plot of data from before the change and saw no large differences in the shape of the two distributions. We must now compare the sigma before and after the change.

FIGURE 17–4

Simplified *t* Distribution Table
To Compare a Sample Average (Size = *n*) to a Population
Average, or to Compare Two Samples of Size n_1 and n_2,
Using $n = (n_1 + n_2 - 1)$

	95% Confidence (Assumes Two-Tailed)		
	If the calculated t_t-test value exceeds the table *t* value, then the two averages being compared are significantly different.		
n	**t value**	**n**	**t value**
6	2.571	31	2.042
7	2.447	32	2.04
8	2.365	33	2.037
9	2.306	34	2.035
10	2.262	35	2.032
11	2.228	36	2.03
12	2.201	37	2.028
13	2.179	38	2.026
14	2.16	39	2.024
15	2.145	40	2.023
16	2.131	45	2.015
17	2.12		
18	2.11	50	2.01
19	2.101		
20	2.093	60	2.001
21	2.086	70	1.995
22	2.08		
23	2.074	80	1.99
24	2.069		
25	2.064	90	1.987
26	2.06	100+	1.984
27	2.056		
28	2.052		
29	2.048		
30	2.045		

What is the minimum sample size we need, assuming we want to be able to see a change *h* of 0.6*S*?

$$h = 0.6S = 0.6 \times 0.00170 \text{ inch} = 0.00102 \text{ inch}$$
$$Z = 1.96$$
$$S = 0.00170 \text{ inch}$$

$$n = \left(\frac{Z * S}{h} \right)^2$$

$$= \left(\frac{1.96 * 0.00170 \text{ inch}}{0.00102 \text{ inch}} \right)^2$$

$$= 11 \qquad \text{(rounding up)}$$

Now that we know the minimum sample size, we can take the sample.

We want to know if the sample sigma is significantly different from the "before" population sigma. Assume that, from the sample, we calculate $s = 0.00173$ inch:

$$n = 11$$
$$s = 0.00173 \text{ inch}$$
$$S = 0.00170 \text{ inch}$$
$$\text{Chi}_t^2 = \frac{(n-1)\,s^2}{S^2} = \frac{(11-1)\,0.00173 \text{ inch}^2}{0.00170 \text{ inch}^2} = 10.356$$

Looking at the Simplified Chi-Square Distribution Table in Figure 17–3, with $n = 11$, the low value is 3.24696, and the high value is 20.4832. Since our test value 10.356 is not outside that range, we can't say that the sigma of the sample is different (at 95 percent confidence) from the population sigma.

Since we were not able to see a difference in the distribution or the sigma, we will now see if the averages are significantly different. Assume that the after-change sample ($n = 11$) had an average $\bar{x}$ of 0.9991 inch:

$$\bar{x} = 0.9991 \text{ inch}$$
$$\bar{X} = 1.0003 \text{ inches}$$
$$s = 0.00173 \text{ inch}$$
$$n = 11$$

$$t_t = \frac{|\bar{x} - \bar{X}|}{\frac{s}{\sqrt{n}}}$$

$$= \frac{|0.9991 \text{ inch} - 1.0003 \text{ inches}|}{\frac{0.00173 \text{ inch}}{\sqrt{11}}} = 2.3005$$

Looking at the Simplified t Distribution Table in Figure 17–4, with $n = 11$, our calculated t-test value 2.3005 is greater than the table value (opposite $n = 11$: 2.228). We therefore assume that, with 95 percent confidence, the sample average *is* significantly different from the population.

The average has changed significantly from what it was before. We should therefore decide whether the process change was detrimental and should be reversed. Here is where judgment must be used, but you have data to help.

CHECKING FOR A SIGNIFICANT CHANGE BETWEEN TWO SAMPLES

We sometimes want to compare samples from two similar processes or from one process at different times. As in comparing a sample to a population, we do three steps in checking for a change between two samples.

1. Check the distributions to see if they are substantially different.
2. If the distribution shapes are not substantially different, then see if the sigmas are significantly different.
3. If neither of the above tests shows a difference, then check if the averages are significantly different.

If we see a difference in any of the above steps, it is important to know since it affects costs, quality, and so on.

1. Checking the Distributions

First, it may be necessary to plot a large number of individual measurements to verify that the sample distribution shapes are similar. Although a process distribution will normally be similar over time, it is important to verify this, especially when running a test, after a policy change, machine wreck, personnel change, and so on. We are only concerned with gross differences, like one plot being very strongly skewed or bimodal versus the other. If plotting is required, it will need a sample size of at least 36. If there is a substantial change in the distribution, we know the process has changed, and we should be trying to understand the change cause and ramifications.

2. Checking the Sigmas

If the sample distributions have not changed qualitatively (looking at the data plots), then you can do some quantitative tests. The first thing to check is if the sigma has changed significantly. The sigma on a process does not normally change unless a substantial basic change in the process has occurred. To see if the sigma has changed we do an *F test*.

FORMULA

F Test Comparing the Sigmas *s* of Two Samples

$$F_t = \frac{s_1^2}{s_2^2} \qquad \text{(Put the larger } s \text{ on top, as the numerator.)}$$

s_1 = sample with the larger sigma
s_2 = sample with the smaller sigma

The sample sizes *n* should be within 20 percent of each other. There are tables and programs that allow for greater differences, but since you control sample sizes and get more reliable results with similar sample sizes, these other tables and programs are generally not needed.

Compare this F_t to the value in the Simplified *F* Table in Figure 17–5. If the F_t value exceeds the table *F* value, then the sigmas are significantly different.

Problem 7

Suppose that in our now-familiar shaft example we take two samples. The samples could be from one lathe or from two different lathes doing the same job. We have already plotted the samples and found that the shapes of the distributions were not substantially different. We now want to know if the sample sigmas are significantly different with 95 percent confidence.

Sample 1	Sample 2
$\bar{x}_1 = 0.9982$ inch	$\bar{x}_2 = 1.0006$ inches
$s_1 = 0.00273$ inch	$s_2 = 0.00162$ inch
$n_1 = 21$	$n_2 = 19$

As before, we must first check the sigmas to see if the two processes are significantly different. We therefore calculate the *F*-test value and compare this to the value in the Simplified *F* Table (Figure 17–5).

FIGURE 17–5

Simplified F Table
95 Percent Confidence. To Compare Sigmas from Two
Samples (Sizes n_1 and n_2, Sizes Equal within 20 Percent)
Using $n = (n_1 + n_2)/2$

		If the calculated F_t value exceeds the table value, assume a significant difference.		
n	*F*		*n*	*F*
6	5.05		31	1.84
7	4.28		32	1.82
8	3.79		33	1.8
9	3.44		34	1.79
10	3.18		35	1.77
11	2.98		36	1.76
12	2.82		37	1.74
13	2.69		38	1.73
14	2.58		39	1.72
15	2.48		40	1.7
16	2.4		42	1.68
17	2.33		44	1.66
18	2.27		46	1.64
19	2.22		48	1.62
20	2.17		50	1.61
21	2.12		60	1.54
22	2.08		70	1.49
23	2.05		80	1.45
24	2.01		100	1.39
25	1.98		120	1.35
26	1.96		150	1.31
27	1.93		200	1.26
28	1.9		300	1.21
29	1.88		400	1.18
30	1.86		500	1.16
			750	1.13
			1000	1.11
			2000	1.08

Since our sample sizes are within 20 percent of each other, we can use the previous formula.

$$F_t = \frac{s_1^2}{s_2^2} = \frac{0.00273 \text{ inch}^2}{0.00162 \text{ inch}^2} = 2.840$$

We now compare 2.840 to the value in the Simplified F Table (Figure 17–5). Use the average $n = 20$ to find the table value, which is 2.17. Since our calculated value is greater than the table value, we can say with 95 percent confidence that the two processes' sigmas are different. We must now decide what the cause and ramifications are of this change in the sigma.

Problem 8

Suppose that in our shaft example we take two different samples. The samples could be from one lathe or from two different lathes doing the same job.

We have already plotted the samples and have found that the distributions are not substantially different. We now want to know if the sample sigmas are significantly different with 95 percent confidence.

Sample 1	Sample 2
$\bar{x}_1 = 0.9982$ inch	$\bar{x}_2 = 1.0006$ inches
$s_1 = 0.00193$ inch	$s_2 = 0.00162$ inch
$n_1 = 21$	$n_2 = 19$

Calculating an F_t:

$$F_t = \frac{s_1^2}{s_2^2} = \frac{0.00193^2}{0.00162^2} = 1.42$$

We now compare 1.42 to the value in the Simplified F Table (Figure 17–5). Use the average $n = 20$ to find the table value, which is 2.17. Since 1.42 is less than the table value of 2.17, we can't say with 95 percent confidence that the processes are different (with regards to their sigmas).

We now test to see if the two sample averages are significantly different.

3. Checking the Averages

Since we did *not* find that either the distribution shape or sigma had changed, we now test whether the two sample averages are significantly different. We calculate a *t-test value* (t_t) to compare to a value in the Simplified t Distribution Table (Figure 17–4).

FORMULA

t Test of Two Sample Averages $\bar{x}_1$ and $\bar{x}_2$

$$t_t = \frac{|\bar{x}_1 - \bar{x}_2|}{\sqrt{\left(\dfrac{n_1 s_1^2 + n_2 s_2^2}{n_1 + n_2}\right)\left(\dfrac{1}{n_1} + \dfrac{1}{n_2}\right)}}$$

$\bar{x}_1$ and $\bar{x}_2$ are two sample averages.

s_1 and s_2 are the sigmas on the two samples.

n_1 and n_2 are the two sample sizes.

$|\bar{x}_1 - \bar{x}_2|$ is the absolute difference between the averages, ignoring a minus sign in the difference.

We then compare this calculated *t*-test value against the value in the Simplified *t* Distribution Table (Figure 17–4). If our calculated *t*-test number is greater than the value in the table, then we are 95 percent confident that the sample averages are significantly different.

Returning to Problem 8, we must calculate our test t_t:

$$\bar{x}_1 = 0.9982 \text{ inch} \qquad \bar{x}_2 = 1.0006 \text{ inches}$$
$$s_1 = 0.00193 \text{ inch} \qquad s_2 = 0.00162 \text{ inch}$$
$$n_1 = 21 \qquad n_2 = 19$$

$$t_t = \frac{|\bar{x}_1 - \bar{x}_2|}{\sqrt{\left(\dfrac{n_1 s_1^2 + n_2 s_2^2}{n_1 + n_2}\right)\left(\dfrac{1}{n_1} + \dfrac{1}{n_2}\right)}}$$

$$= \frac{|0.9982 \text{ inch} - 1.0006 \text{ inches}|}{\sqrt{\left(\dfrac{21(0.00193 \text{ inch})^2 + 19(0.00162 \text{ inch})^2}{21 + 19}\right)\left(\dfrac{1}{21} + \dfrac{1}{19}\right)}} = 4.24$$

We now compare this 4.24 with the value from the Simplified *t* Distribution Table (Figure 17–4). (Use $n = n_1 + n_2 - 1 = 39$.) Since the calculated 4.24 is greater than the table value of 2.024, we can conclude with 95 percent confidence that the two process means are significantly different.

We would normally want to find out why and decide what we are going to do with this knowledge.

> **TIP**
>
> Tests on averages and sigmas never prove "sameness."
>
> The chi-square, F, and t tests test only for significant difference. If these tests do not show a significant difference, it does not prove that the two samples or the sample and population are identical. It just means that with the amount of data we have, we can't conclude with 95 percent confidence that they are different. *Confidence tests never prove that two things are the same!*

INCIDENTAL STATISTICS TERMINOLOGY NOT USED IN THE PRECEDING TESTS

You will not find the term *null hypothesis* used in the above confidence tests, but it is inferred by the way the tests are done. *Null hypothesis* is a term that is often used in statistics books to mean that the base assumption is that nothing (null) changed. (An analogy is someone's being assumed innocent until proven guilty.)

This assumption is included in the above tests, and it is the basis for the above Tip that the hypothesis tests never prove "sameness." (Again, just because a person is not proven guilty does not necessarily mean that he or she is innocent.) There is no need to add the complexity of the term *null hypothesis* when the nature of the tests implies it.

Several of the tables used in this book are titled as "simplified." This includes the chi-square, F, and t tables. The main simplification relates to the column showing sample size n. In most other statistics books, the equivalent chi-square, F, and t tables label this column as *degrees of freedom*. One statistics book states that degrees of freedom is one of the most difficult terms in statistics to describe. The statistics book then goes on to show that, in almost all cases, degrees of freedom is equivalent to $n - 1$. This therefore becomes the knee-jerk translation ($n - 1 =$ degrees of freedom) of almost everyone using tables with degrees of freedom.

The chi-square, F, and t tables in this book are shown with the $n - 1$ equivalency built in. This was done to make life easier. In the extremely rare cases where degrees of freedom is not equivalent to $n - 1$, the resultant error will be trivial versus the accuracy requirements of the results. The validity of your Six Sigma test results will not be compromised.

You may need this ($n - 1$ = degrees of freedom) equivalency if you refer to other tables or use software with degrees of freedom requested.

At the beginning of this chapter we showed two groups of data related to the price/earnings ratios of stocks and said that we would come back to this data later. Now we have all the formulas we need to compare these two data samples to see if they are significantly different, and therefore make some judgment, at 95 percent confidence, whether the populations from which these samples were drawn were different. Assume that we have plotted samples from both populations and are comfortable that the two populations have similar distributions. Here, again, are the two sets of data, with their averages and standard deviations:

Two Sets of Data on Stock Price/Earnings Ratios

	Group 1	Group 2
	20.3	18.8
	19.5	17.7
	23.8	23.4
	16.9	22.9
	20.1	22.0
	27.4	19.8
	22.4	18.5
	25.3	24.0
	18.7	24.8
	23.5	17.5
	27.3	15.5
	21.0	21.2
	18.0	26.8
	24.8	25.1
	23.6	18.3
Average	22.173	21.087
Standard deviation	3.278	3.353

So,

Sample 1	Sample 2
$\bar{x}_1 = 22.173$	$\bar{x}_2 = 21.087$
$s_1 = 3.278$	$s_2 = 3.353$
$n_1 = 15$	$n_2 = 15$

We must first check the sigmas to see if the two processes are significantly different. We therefore calculate an F-test value, and we compare this to the value in the Simplified F Table (Figure 17–5).

Since our sample sizes are within 20 percent of each other, we can use the following formula:

$$F_t = \frac{s_1^2}{s_2^2} = \frac{11.243}{10.745} = 1.046$$

We now compare 1.046 to the value in the Simplified F Table (Figure 17–5). We use the average $n = 15$ to find the table value, which is 2.48. Since our calculated value is not greater than the table value, we can't say with 95 percent confidence that the two processes' sigmas are statistically significantly different.

We now test to see if the two samples' averages are significantly different.

We calculate a *t-test value* (t_t) to compare to a value in the Simplified t Distribution Table (Figure 17–4):

$$t_t = \frac{|\bar{x}_1 - \bar{x}_2|}{\sqrt{\left(\frac{n_1 s_1^2 + n_2 s_2^2}{n_1 + n_2}\right)\left(\frac{1}{n_1} + \frac{1}{n_2}\right)}}$$

$$= \frac{1.086}{1.211} = 0.897$$

We now compare this 0.897 with the value from the Simplified t Distribution Table (Figure 17–4). (We use $n = n_1 + n_2 - 1 = 29$.) Since the calculated 0.897 is not greater than the table value of 2.048, we can't conclude with 95 percent confidence that the two process means are statistically significantly different.

We therefore can't conclude with 95 percent confidence that the price/earnings ratio of the stocks from which the Group 1 sample was drawn is any different than the price/earnings ratio of the stocks from which the Group 2 sample was drawn.

This result emphasizes why we can't, without some analysis, just use the sample averages and standard deviations to make a judgment related to their respective populations. We must always do additional analysis to see if the numerical differences are statistically significant.

CHAPTER 17 REVIEW

1. Valid sampling and analysis of variables data are needed for the Define, Measurement, Analysis, and Control steps in the DMAIC process.
2. Variables data are usually in decimal form. Resolution must be such that at least 10 measurement steps are within the tolerance or within the area of interest.
3. The rule-of-thumb minimum sample size on variables data is 11.
4. When possible, use the formulas to determine minimum sample size.
5. We seldom have complete data on a population, but we can use samples to estimate its composition.
6. The greater the sample size, the better the estimate on the population.
7. Sample size is usually a compromise between cost and desire for accuracy.
8. We normally work to 95 percent confidence test level.
9. Assume a problem is two-tailed (high *and* low) unless it has been described specifically as one-tailed.
10. We normally want to sense a change equal to 10 percent of the tolerance or 0.6S.
11. When checking for a change, we can compare a sample with earlier population data or compare two samples with each other.
12. We follow a three-step process when analyzing for change. Compare distribution shapes first, then sigma, and then averages. If significant change is identified at any step in the process, we stop. We then must decide what to do with the knowledge that the process changed.
13. Change analysis is useful on any process or population where data are available.

Testing for Statistically Significant Change Using Proportional Data

In this chapter we will learn to use limited samples on proportional data. This chapter will parallel the last chapter, in which we learned to use limited samples on variables data. Valid sampling and analysis of proportional data may be needed in all steps in the DMAIC process.

When a news report discusses the latest poll taken on 1,000 people related to two presidential hopefuls, and one candidate gets 51 percent and the other 49 percent of the votes, a knowledgeable news reporter will *not* say that one candidate is ahead. This is because the poll results are merely an *estimate* on the overall population's choice for president and the sample poll results have to be significantly different before any conclusion can be made as to what the total population is expected to vote. In this chapter you will learn how large of a sample is required and what difference in sample results is needed before we can predict, with 95 percent confidence, that there are true differences in a population.

Changes in Real Processes, Proportional Data

Manufacturing
Use samples of scrap parts to calculate proportions on shifts or similar production lines. Look for statistically significant differences in scrap rate.

Sales
Sample and compare proportions of successful sales by different salespeople.

Marketing
Use polls to prioritize where advertising dollars should be spent.

Accounting and Software Development
Use samples to compare error rates of groups or individuals.

Receivables
Sample overdue receivables, then compare proportions versus due dates on different product lines. Adjust prices on products with statistically different overdue receivables.

Insurance
Sample challenged claims versus total claims in different groups, then compare proportions. Adjust group prices accordingly.

DEFINITION

proportional data   Proportional data are based on attribute inputs such as good or bad or yes or no. Examples are the proportion of defects in a process, proportion of yes votes for a candidate, and the proportion of students failing a test.

Proportional data can also be based on "stepped" numerical data, where the measurements steps are too wide to use as attribute data.

TIP

Because of the large sample sizes required when using proportional data, if possible use variables data instead.

When people are interviewed regarding their preference in an upcoming election, the outcome of the sampling is proportional data. The interviewer asks whether a person is intending to vote for a candidate, yes or no. After polling many people, the pollsters tabulate the proportion of yes (or no) results versus the total number of people surveyed. This kind of data requires very large sample sizes. That is why pollsters state that, based on polling over 1,000 people, the predictions are accurate within 3 percent or ±3 percent (with 95 percent confidence). We will be able to validate this with the following sample size formula.

FORMULA

Calculating Minimum Sample Size and Sensitivity, Proportional Data

$$n = \left[\frac{1.96\sqrt{(p)(1-p)}}{h} \right]^2$$

n = sample size of attribute data, like good and bad (95 percent confidence)

p = probability of an event (the proportion of bad in a sample, chance of getting elected, and so on) (When in doubt, use $p = 0.5$, the most conservative.)

h = sensitivity, or accuracy required (For example, for predicting elections, it may be ±3 percent or $h = 0.03$. Another guideline is to be able to sense 10 percent of the tolerance or difference between the proportions.)

Note that the formula shown above can be rewritten:

$$h = 1.96\sqrt{\frac{(p)(1-p)}{n}}$$

This allows us to see what sensitivity h we will be able to sense at a given sample size and probability.

Let's do an election example. If the most recent polls show that a candidate has a 20 percent chance of getting elected, we may use $p = 0.2$. We will want an accuracy of ±3 percent of the total vote, so $h = 0.03$.

$$p = 0.2$$
$$h = 0.03$$
$$n = \left[\frac{1.96\sqrt{(p)(1-p)}}{h} \right]^2$$
$$= \left[\frac{1.96\sqrt{(0.2)(1-0.2)}}{0.03} \right]^2$$
$$= 682.95$$

So we would have to poll 683 (round up) people to get an updated probability on someone whose estimated chance of being elected was 20 percent in earlier polls. However, if we had no polls to estimate a candidate's chances or we wanted to be the most conservative, we would use $p = 0.5$.

$$p = 0.5$$
$$h = 0.03$$

$$n = \left[\frac{1.96\sqrt{(p)(1-p)}}{h} \right]^2$$

$$= \left[\frac{1.96\sqrt{(0.5)(1-0.5)}}{0.03} \right]^2$$

$$= 1{,}067.1$$

In this case, with $p = 0.5$, we would need to poll 1,068 (round up) people to be within 3 percent in estimating the chance of the candidate's being elected.

As you can see, the sample size of 683, with $p = 0.2$, is quite a bit less than the 1,068 required with $p = 0.5$. Since earlier polls may no longer be valid, most pollsters use the 1,068 as a standard. Using this formula, we have verified the pollsters requiring over 1,000 inputs on a close election to be within 3 percent on forecasting the election outcome with 95 percent confidence.

Equally, because the forecast has only 95 percent confidence, the prediction can be wrong 5 percent of the time!

In some cases we have a choice of getting variables or attribute data. Many companies choose to use go/no-go gauges for checking parts. This choice is made because go/no-go gauges are often easier to use than a variables gauge that gives measurement data. However, a go/no-go gauge checks only whether a part is within tolerance, either good or bad, and it gives no indication as to *how* good or *how* bad a part is. This generates attribute data that are then used to calculate proportions.

Any process improvement with proportions is far more difficult because it requires much larger sample sizes than the variables data used in the examples in the previous chapter. Using a gauge that gives variables (measurement) data output is a better choice!

With proportional data, comparing samples or a sample versus the population involves comparing ratios normally stated as decimals. These comparisons can be can be expressed in units of defects per hundred or of any other criterion that is consistent with both the sample and population. Although these proportions can be stated as decimals, the individual inputs are still attributes.

FORMULA

Comparing a Proportional Sample with the Population (95 Percent Confidence)

First, we must calculate a test value Z_t:

$$Z_t = \frac{|p - P|}{\sqrt{\dfrac{P(1 - P)}{n}}}$$

P = proportion of defects (or whatever) in the population
p = proportion of defects (or same as above) in the sample
$|p - P|$ = absolute proportion difference (no minus sign in difference)
n = sample size

If $Z_t > 1.96$, then we can say with 95 percent confidence that the sample is statistically different from the population.

Following is the formula for comparing two proportional data samples to each other. We will then show a case study that incorporates the formulas for proportional data sample size, comparing a proportion sample with the population and comparing two proportion samples with each other.

FORMULA

Comparing Two Proportional Data Samples (95 Percent Confidence)

Calculate a test value Z_t:

$$Z_t = \frac{\left|\dfrac{x_1}{n_1} - \dfrac{x_2}{n_2}\right|}{\sqrt{\left(\dfrac{x_1 + x_2}{n_1 + n_2}\right)\left(1 - \dfrac{x_1 + x_2}{n_1 + n_2}\right)\left(\dfrac{1}{n_1} + \dfrac{1}{n_2}\right)}}$$

x_1 = number of defects (or whatever) in sample 1
x_2 = number of defects (or same as above) in sample 2
$\left|\dfrac{x_1}{n_1} - \dfrac{x_2}{n_2}\right|$ = absolute proportion difference (no minus sign in difference)
n_1 = size of sample 1
n_2 = size of sample 2

If $Z_t > 1.96$, then we can say with 95 percent confidence that the two samples are significantly different.

Case Study: Source of Crack

Glass lenses were being automatically packed by a machine. The lenses were then shipped to another plant where they were assembled into a final consumer product. The assembly machine in the other plant would jam if a lens broke, and 0.1 percent of the lenses were breaking during assembly, which was causing excessive down-time. The assembly plant management suspected that the lenses were being cracked during the automatic packing process at the lens plant and that these cracks would then break during assembly.

In order to test this theory, management decided to run a test in which half the lenses would be randomly packed manually while the other half was being packed automatically. This randomness would make the lens population quality the same in both groups of packed lenses.

They decided to use a test sensitivity of 50 percent for the difference between the two samples because they believed that the automatic packer was the dominant source of the cracks and that the difference between the two packed samples would be dramatic. Even with this sensitivity, the calculated minimum sample size was 15,352 manually packed lenses!

The tests were run, with 15,500 lenses being manually packed and 15,500 lenses being auto packed.

The results were that 12 of the automatically packed lenses and 4 of the manually packed lenses broke when assembled. Management determined that this difference was statistically significant. Because of the costs involved of rebuilding the packer, they reran the test, and the results were similar.

The automatic packer was rebuilt, and the problem of the lenses' breaking in the assembly operation was no longer an issue.

Since the above case study incorporates all of the formulas we have covered in the use of samples on proportional data, we will use a series of problems to review in detail how the case study decisions were reached.

Problem 1

Assuming we wish to be able to sense a 50 percent defect difference between two proportional data samples, and the historical defect level is 0.1 percent, what is the minimum number of samples we must study? Assume 95 percent confidence.

$$p = 0.001$$
$$h = 0.0005 \text{ (which is 50 percent of } p\text{)}$$
$$n = \left[\frac{1.96\sqrt{(p)(1-p)}}{h} \right]^2$$

$$= \left[\frac{1.96\sqrt{(0.001)(1-0.001)}}{0.0005} \right]^2$$

$$= 15{,}352 \qquad \text{(Round up.)}$$

Answer: We would have to check 15,352 components to have 95 percent confidence that we could see a change of 0.05 percent.

Problem 2

Of 15,500 automatically packed lenses, 12 broke during assembly. Of 15,500 manually packed test lenses, 4 broke during assembly. Is the manually packed sample breakage statistically significantly different from the breakage in the auto packed sample?

$x_1 = 12$

$x_2 = 4$

$n_1 = 15{,}500$

$n_2 = 15{,}500$

$$Z_t = \frac{\left| \dfrac{x_1}{n_1} - \dfrac{x_2}{n_2} \right|}{\sqrt{\left(\dfrac{x_1 + x_2}{n_1 + n_2} \right)\left(1 - \dfrac{x_1 + x_2}{n_1 + n_2} \right)\left(\dfrac{1}{n_1} + \dfrac{1}{n_2} \right)}}$$

$$= \frac{\left| \dfrac{12}{15{,}500} - \dfrac{4}{15{,}500} \right|}{\sqrt{\left(\dfrac{12 + 4}{15{,}500 + 15{,}500} \right)\left(1 - \dfrac{12 + 4}{15{,}500 + 15{,}500} \right)\left(\dfrac{1}{15{,}500} + \dfrac{1}{15{,}500} \right)}}$$

$$= 2.001$$

Answer: Since 2.001 is greater than the test value of 1.96, we can say with 95 percent confidence that the manual pack test sample is significantly different from the baseline sample.

Because of the cost of rebuilding the packer, the test was rerun with similar results. The decision was then made to rebuild the packer.

Just for interest, after the packer was rebuilt, the test was run a third time. In this case the automatic packer had zero defects, whereas the manual pack still had some defects. Apparently the manual packing was not as gentle as assumed, and it was causing some cracks.

In the previous chapter, we indicated that numerical data cannot be analyzed as variables if the discrimination is such that there are fewer than 10 steps within the range of interest. One of the example data sets had ages in whole years for a five-year period. Let's do a problem assuming we had such a data set, analyzing it as proportional data.

Problem 3

A health study was being done on a group of men aged 50 to 55. Each man in the study had filled out a questionnaire related to his health. The men gave their ages in whole years. One of the questions on the questionnaire asked whether they had seen a doctor within the previous year.

One element of the study was to ascertain whether the men in the study who were 55 years of age had seen a doctor in the last year more often than the others in the study. The people doing the study wanted to be able to sense a difference of 3 percent at a 95 percent confidence level.

This problem will involve comparing two proportions: the proportion of 55-year-old men who had seen a doctor in the last year and the proportion of 50- through 54-year-old men who had seen a doctor in the last year.

Since the number of men in the age 50- through 54-year-old group is much larger than the age 55 group, we will use that larger group as a population. (Note that this problem could also be solved as a comparison between two samples).

We first determine the minimum sample size:

$p = 0.5$ (The probability of having seen a doctor within the last year. Without additional information, this is the most conservative.)

$h = 0.03$

$$n = \left[\frac{1.96\sqrt{(p)(1-p)}}{h} \right]^2$$

$$= \left[\frac{1.96\sqrt{(0.5)(1-0.5)}}{0.03} \right]^2$$

$$= 1{,}067.1$$

So the study must have at least 1,068 men 55 years of age.

Assume that the study had 1,500 men 55 years of age, which is more than the 1,068 minimum. There were 5,000 men aged 50 through 54. The questionnaire indicated that 828 of the men aged 55 had seen the doctor in the last year and 2,650 of the men aged 50 through 54 had seen a doctor:

$$Z_t = \frac{|p - P|}{\sqrt{\dfrac{P(1-P)}{n}}}$$

$P = 2650/5000 = 0.5300$ (Proportion of the study population aged 50 through 54 who had seen a doctor in the prior year)

$p = 828/1500 = 0.5520$ (Proportion in the age 55 group who had seen a doctor in the prior year)

$|p - P| = 0.02200$

$n = 1{,}500$

$Z_t = 0.02200/0.01289 = 1.707$

Since 1.707 is not greater than 1.96, we can't say with 95 percent confidence that the men aged 55 saw a doctor in the last year at a higher rate than the men aged 50 through 54.

CHAPTER 18 REVIEW

1. Valid sampling and analysis of proportional data may be needed for all the steps in the DMAIC process.

2. Proportional data are generated from attribute inputs such as yes or no and go/no-go, or from "stepped" numerical data with wide steps.

3. Testing for statistically significant change with proportional data involves comparing proportions, or ratios, stated as decimals.

4. Proportional data require much larger sample sizes than variables data.

5. Sample size is usually a compromise between cost and desire for accuracy.

6. We normally work to a 95 percent confidence level.

7. We generally want to be able to sense a change of 10 percent of the difference between the proportions or 10 percent of the tolerance.

8. When checking for a change, we can compare a sample with population data or compare two samples with each other.

9. Change analysis using proportional data is useful anywhere we have proportions but don't have variables data.

CHAPTER 19

Testing for Statistically Significant Change in Nonnormal Distributions

What we will learn in this chapter is that many distributions are nonnormal and they occur in many places. But we can use the formulas and tables we have already reviewed to get meaningful information on any changes in the processes that generated these distributions. We often conduct Six Sigma work on nonnormal processes.

Nonnormal Distributions Are Not Unusual, and They Occur in Many Places

Manufacturing
Any process having a zero at one end of the data is likely to have a skewed distribution. An example would be data representing distortion on a product.

Sales
If your salespeople tend to be made up of two distinct groups, one group experienced and the other inexperienced, the data distribution showing sales versus age is likely to be bimodal.

Marketing
The data showing dollars spent in different markets may be nonnormal because of a focus on specific markets.

Accounting and Software Development
Error rate data may be strongly skewed based on the complexity or uniqueness of a program or accounting procedure.

Receivables
Delinquent receivables may be skewed based on the product or service involved.

Insurance
Costs at treatment centers in different cities may be nonnormal because of varying labor rates.

In the real world, nonnormal distributions are commonplace. Figure 19–1 gives some examples. Note that the plots in the figure are of the individual parts measurements. These are some examples of where these would occur:

- The *uniform distribution* would occur if you plotted the numbers occurring from spinning a roulette wheel or from rolling a single die.
- The *skewed distribution* would be a typical result of a one-sided process, such as the of nonflatness or positive warp on a machined part. Zero may be one end of the chart.
- The *bimodal distribution* can occur when there is play in a piece of equipment or where a process has a self-correcting feedback loop. This distribution could also indicate that there are two independent processes involved.

In most classes on Six Sigma, one of the statistical tests is to check the plotted data to see if it is normal. However, it often seems that, no matter what the outcome of this test, the analysis of the data proceeds as if the data were completely normal. For most Six Sigma work, this is not a serious problem. Here is why.

If the population is not normal, then the absolute probabilities generated from using computer programs or from tables may be somewhat in error. This would include results obtained from using the Standardized Normal Distribution Table (Figure 16–6). If we want to have good estimates of the *absolute* probabilities, the population must be normal for us to use it on any computer program or table based on a normal distribution.

FIGURE 19–1

Nonnormal Distribution Examples

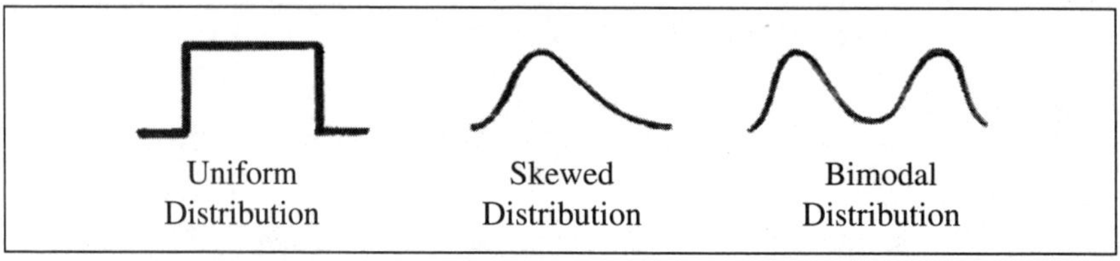

| Uniform Distribution | Skewed Distribution | Bimodal Distribution |

TIP

Statistical Tests on Variables, Nonnormal Data

You can use the statistical tests in this book for evaluating change, including referencing the numbers in the Standardized Normal Distribution Table (Figure 16–6), to compare a process before and after a change, or to compare processes with similarly shaped nonnormal distributions. However, it is important to know that, although the *relative qualitative comparison is valid*, the absolute probability values on each process may be somewhat inaccurate.

As in checking processes with normal distributions, the distributions that are nonnormal must be periodically plotted to verify that the shapes of the distributions are still similar. If a distribution shape has changed dramatically, you can't use the formulas or charts in this book for before and after comparisons. It would be the proverbial apples-versus-oranges thing! However, similar processes usually have and keep similarly shaped distributions.

However, since most of the work we do in Six Sigma involves *comparing similar processes relatively* (before and after or between two similar processes) to see if we have made a significant change, these *relative* comparisons are valid even if the data we are using are nonnormal.

There are esoteric statistics based on nonnormal distributions and software packages that will give more accurate estimates of actual probabilities, but they require that the user be very knowledgeable in statistics. This added degree of accuracy is not required for most Six Sigma work where we are looking for significant change, not absolute defect values.

Not verifying that a distribution shape stays consistent can cause costly errors, and not just in manufacturing. Let's say that you are active in playing the stock market, and you have plotted the price/earnings ratios for a spectrum of stocks. Your data have come from several years when the stock market was fairly stable, the distribution appears normal, and you are going to use these data in your decision-making process on whether to buy or sell stocks.

Then the market enters into a strong upward trend—a "bull market." Unless you replot the data, you will not be aware that you are now likely to have a "fat" upper tail on the distribution—that is, a skewed distribution, with an unexpectedly large number of stocks having very high price/earnings ratios. The distribution has changed and is no longer normal. This is because in a bull market many people "buy high."

The reverse happens in a down, or "bear," market. The tail on the low end of the distribution becomes fat—a disproportionate number of stocks are sold at unusually low prices versus their earnings.

Indeed, many people *do* buy high in bull markets and then sell low when the market drops.

If you were using the distribution of data you had taken during the stable market period to make decisions during the bull or bear markets, you could very well have joined the masses in buying high and selling low!

The above-mentioned masses are not the only ones to erroneously assume that the world, and its distributions, stays the same. In 1994, Bill Krasker and John Meriwether, two winners of the Nobel Prize for Economics, started a company called Long-Term Capital Management (LTCM). These two "geniuses" conducted massive data analysis on the "spreads" between various financial instruments, like corporate bonds and Treasury bonds. When these spreads got wider than what was statistically expected (based on their computer program), LTCM would buy the financial instrument likely to gain from the correction that was expected to occur shortly.

Using this methodology, LTCM was unbelievably successful for four years. By leveraging their money, they gained as much as 40 percent per year for their investors, and Bill Krasker and John Meriwether became very wealthy.

They were so successful that by 1998 LTCM had $1 trillion in leveraged exposure in various financial market positions. But LTCM then became a victim of the fat-tail phenomenon. It so happened that everyone who had been playing in similar financial markets all decided to get out at once, and LTCM saw results that their computer models had predicted would *not statistically happen in more than a billion years*! However, unbeknownst to them, the distribution had changed, which made the earlier computer-generated probability prediction invalid.

The risks that LTCM had taken were so dangerous that LTCM was close to upsetting the whole world's financial institutions.

Several of the world's major banks got together and successfully stopped this potential global financial disaster by giving additional credit to LTCM.

The two geniuses still lost over $4 billion, and the relaxed credit that was established by the banks to save LTCM then enabled companies like Enron to do their thing—but that is a separate story and book! However, this example underscores the importance of plotting distributions to be sure that they have not changed.

CHAPTER 19 REVIEW

1. We often conduct Six Sigma work on nonnormal processes.
2. You can use the statistical tests in this book for calculating differences on similarly shaped nonnormal distributions.
3. The absolute probability values obtained may be somewhat inaccurate, but comparing probabilities to determine qualitative change on a process or on similar processes is valid.
4. As in checking processes with normal distributions, the distributions that are nonnormal must be periodically plotted to verify that the shapes of the distributions are still similar. You cannot use standard numerical statistical tests to compare differently shaped distributions.
5. Any distribution with a nonnormal shape should be analyzed for cause. If the cause is not obvious, then an investigation should follow. Often large gains come from these surprise observations.

PART SIX

Controlling a Process and Teaching Six Sigma

Munit haec et altera vincit.   (One defends and the other conquers.)

—Latin saying

Once a process is in control, it is imperative to *keep* the process in control. Chapter 20 describes ways of making improvements that are robust and therefore less likely to go out of control.

Anyone who runs a Six Sigma project will have some involvement in teaching the Six Sigma methodology. Chapter 21 covers some of the issues or challenges you may face in this instruction.

Keeping a Process in Control

In this chapter we will discuss different ways to keep a process in control and the related challenges. This chapter applies to the Control step in the DMAIC process.

The earlier chapters discussed the means of improving a process or product. However, some improvements are eventually forgotten or ignored, and the process is put back to the way it was before the change. To avoid backsliding, process control is essential.

Case Study: Retro Forming Equipment

A manufacturing plant was having an issue with a product dimension that was generated by a specific forming tool, and they were reviewing the issue with a team of engineers from their home office engineering group. One of the engineers from this team had worked with this plant for a large number of years, and he recalled that many years before the plant had experienced a similar issue. He remembered that the solution was a slight dimensional change in the forming tool. He was sure that the change had been documented and that the revised forming tool had a different part number that was stamped into the tool face.

The engineer was able to get the revised forming tool part number from the company's engineering records, and so he went out onto the production floor to make sure that the proper forming tool was being used.

On looking at the stamped number on the forming tool that was being used, the engineer found that the tool was an older version, without the update. Talking to the person who inventoried the plant's equipment, he discovered that this person was relatively new to the job. Unbeknownst to this person, the inventory still had some old forming tools that looked almost identical to the new tools. Without carefully verifying the stamped number, which the new employee was not doing, it was easy to pick an outdated tool.

On trying to understand why the plant had these old tools after all these years, the engineer discovered that many of the "old-timers" had concluded, from their experience, that changes were often reversed, so they kept the old equipment just in case!

The engineer had the inventory employee, in the engineer's presence, find all the old forming tools and destroy them. This resolved the problem.

The above case study shows the difficulty of keeping a process change in control. Whoever had implemented the initial forming tool change had made a very specific mechanical change, changed the engineering drawing, ordered a supply of replacement parts, and directed that the new part be used. However, it wasn't clear whether specific instructions were given to destroy the old equipment or if this instruction had been given but had not been verified. Many years later this old equipment came back to haunt them. It is important to cover every possibility of error because Murphy is lurking!

It is impossible to make an all-inclusive list of control details because they vary so much with the project or process involved. However, here are some general guidelines:

- Communication on the change detail and rationale is critical on *every* change. This communication must include changing any tolerance, procedure, or data sheet related to the change. Instructions should be given to scrap old drawings or instructions. This measure is not trivial or easy to implement because people often have procedures and prints squirreled away in their own files.

- When possible, make a quantitative physical change that is obvious to all such that the part is visibly different. This could include color coding the new part. Destroy, or make inaccessible, all previous equipment that doesn't include the change.

- If the change is qualitative, then make sure appropriate training, quality checks, gauges and verifications, and operator feedback are in place. If operator feedback is required, make sure the needed dimensional data are given to the operator on a timely basis. Simplified control charts, detailed in *Statistics for Six Sigma Made Easy* (see Related Reading and Software) are an excellent way to communicate these data.

- Be sure that there are no individuals on the project who are not in agreement with the change because they may take actions to subvert the change. Everyone must be onboard *before* implementation.

- For some period of time after the change is implemented, periodically verify that the expected gains are truly occurring. This verification should be done in addition to any regularly scheduled quality checks.

Case Study: Tubing Cutting Improvements Forgotten

In Chapter 6, a QFD was discussed on the development of a method for optimizing the cutting of extruded tubing. The benefits were quantified and the project implemented.

Approximately five years after this project was completed, one of the engineers who had been involved in the initial Six Sigma tubing cutting project was visiting the tubing manufacturing plant on a totally unrelated issue. He noticed that the cutters were no longer running as well as they had been at the completion of the Six Sigma project. He knew that a several-years' follow-up had ascertained that the gains were holding, so he wanted to find out why the cutting process had now deteriorated.

He went to see the plant manager, who had been in his position for only a few months. The plant manager had been promoted from another part of the company, so he wasn't familiar with the plant's past. When the engineer gave his observation that the tubing cutters did not seem to be working correctly, the plant manager's reply was that he also had noticed this but that the operators and engineers in the plant had told him that the cutters had never worked very well.

The visiting engineer then told the plant manager about the Six Sigma tubing cutting project that had been completed five years before, and its apparent success. On querying the plant manager, the engineer found that virtually everyone who had been directly involved with the Six Sigma project at the plant had either retired or quit, and the plant manager said that as far as he knew, the plant had no documentation related to the Six Sigma tubing cutting project.

However, with a few minutes' search, the plant manager *was* able to find multiple copies of the Six Sigma project manual, with all needed detail. The manuals were sitting on a shelf in the office of one of the plant engineers who had retired.

The visiting engineer then bet the plant manager $1 that if the plant took just one tubing cutter and set it up as specified in the Six Sigma manual, that the plant manager would then see that the adjusted tubing cutting devices worked extremely well. The plant manager took the bet.

A week later the engineer received a letter in the mail from the plant manager. It contained two items: a $1 bill and a note with the word "thanks."

Some weeks later, when the engineer again visited the plant, he noticed that all the cutting devices were running well. When he asked the plant manager what had caused the cutters to run poorly, the answer was that it had been a combination of small changes that had crept in over the past year. No one had noticed that each change was slowly deteriorating the cutter's performance. And the people's memory as to the cutters' "never running well" apparently was based on the prior year.

Control is still an issue in Six Sigma, and no one has come up with foolproof answers. GE initially had the works of every Six Sigma project put into an accessible database, which was supposed to resolve this. But very quickly this database became filled with meaningless project detail. Also, many situations evolved over time similarly to that described in the above case study: The plant manager wasn't even aware that a Six Sigma project had been successfully completed on the tubing cutter issue, so he would not have known to access the database.

As plants downsize and staffs are reduced, control becomes an even bigger challenge. As mentioned earlier, the best Six Sigma solutions relate to mechanical changes to a process, with little reliance on people's actions to maintain a gain. There should be a strong emphasis on making improvements that are robust and inherent to the process or equipment rather than being reliant on adjustments by an operator. However, even when equipment changes are the remedy for problems, vigilance is still required to ensure that the changes are maintained.

CHAPTER 20 REVIEW

Long-term control of Six Sigma projects is an issue, especially when the projects involve qualitative improvements. The following guidelines, although not inclusive, will help minimize the control problem:

1. Communication on the change reason and rationale is critical on *every* change. This communication must include changing any tolerance, procedure, or data sheet related to the change.
2. When possible, make a quantitative physical change that is obvious to all. Destroy, or make inaccessible, all previous equipment that has not incorporated the change.
3. If the change is qualitative, then make sure appropriate training, quality checks, gauges and verifications, and operator feedback are in place.

4. Be sure that there are no individuals involved with the project who have not bought in to the change because they may take actions to make the change unsuccessful.

5. For some time period after the change is implemented, verify periodically that the expected gains are truly occurring.

CHAPTER 21

Teaching Six Sigma

This chapter will review details of teaching Six Sigma. Many of you who use this text will become involved in teaching this methodology. The people you will teach will have various educational backgrounds and various interest levels. Perhaps my experiences in teaching Six Sigma will be helpful to you as *you* begin to teach Six Sigma.

I had already been at GE for many years and was managing a successful engineering team when Six Sigma was introduced. GE initially had a limited number of bright people trained by outside consultants deemed expert in Six Sigma. This group of newly trained people then put together a set of modules to be used to train the next group of people, which mostly consisted of managers.

Since these original trainers had no experience in actually using Six Sigma, both the modules and the training were rather haphazard. The training consisted of two one-week sessions, which included introduction to several software packages specific to Six Sigma.

In addition to these class sessions, GE brought in outside consultants who covered additional Six Sigma tools and their corresponding software. Because of the software requirements, many people had to order new computers.

So there was a dichotomy in the training. The homegrown training modules, written and taught by nonexperts in Six Sigma, were often weak. The training conducted by the consultants was often overwhelming. It was problematic that there was no existing practical text to use for teaching Six Sigma.

Over a period of months, this training was given to most of the engineers and to other groups such as marketing and sales. After taking these classes, the people were to start using Six Sigma. The goal was that everyone, within one year, would complete two meaningful Six Sigma projects, document the savings, put in the necessary controls, and prepare a formal presentation. Everyone was also to be given a test at the end of the year on his or her competence in Six Sigma. Those completing this would become green belts.

After most of my engineering team had completed the classes, I asked them for feedback. At first I got the "they were okay" type of response. As I queried further, however, I found that the engineers had not truly learned or understood enough. The major weakness in the instruction was that it gave too much attention to theory and too little attention to practical applications.

Since I took great pride in my team's being one of the best, I decided to start teaching a more practical version of Six Sigma to my team. I proceeded to schedule four-hour Six Sigma sessions with my team every other week, in which I would cover some specific area of Six Sigma. The first sessions were a general review of the Six Sigma methodology, emphasizing only what was needed to actually do Six Sigma work. Then we got into specific Six Sigma tools, simplifying them where applicable. Included in these classes were a review of basic probability and statistics to the level required to do Six Sigma projects. After several months the general manager asked me to start the training over with another team, which I did. Everyone attending the classes became a green belt by the one-year target.

DIVERSITY OF SKILLS

In the classes I had to overcome the problem of a great diversity of skills and abilities. There were participants with two-year technical degrees, nontechnical degrees, engineering degrees, and one person with a doctorate in physics. I explained to all of them that I was going to start with the basics and move slowly, with applied problems as examples. This approach seemed to work. Even those who felt they already had an understanding of Six Sigma were surprised how much they learned from these classes.

How did I prepare for the classes? The weekend before I would get every resource I could find on the subject I was going to cover, then do my best to glean the important points and attempt to present them in an understandable manner. Since the people I was teaching knew me well, feedback (positive and negative) was not an issue. This enabled me to fine-tune the course material. I hope this text will negate the need for you to pursue this level of preparation.

After several months of this, a surge of pride began building in these teams. They were even bragging to other teams that they were going to blow them away on the year-end test (which they did).

Another issue I had to address in these classes was related to a few very skilled individuals who over the years had done well without using Six Sigma. It was a difficult sell to get them to put much effort into learning and applying this methodology. However, these people were bright enough that they were able to get some degree of competence in Six Sigma just by attending the classes.

TRAINING THE CONTRIBUTORS

Another facet of teaching Six Sigma arises when you start to actually use the methodology. You have to provide some training to all the people you will be asking to contribute, even those people who are, for practical purposes, working only at the margins of a particular project. These people must get some feel for the Six Sigma process. An initial meeting of two or three hours is needed before involving them in the process. In the meeting emphasize that Six Sigma needs input from knowledgeable people (them) and that data, which they will help gather, will drive the decisions. Explain that you will be doing some statistical tests on the data and that they don't need to understand all the details, but you will share the results. This means that you also need to have one or two additional meetings with everyone to keep them up to date.

There will be a few people within any group who will want to better understand Six Sigma. There should be additional meetings for these people since they will become your best ambassadors!

When teaching Six Sigma, give a Six Sigma text to each person taking the class or contributing to a Six Sigma project. This would include hourly maintenance people, customers, and so on. In this way, even though you may be teaching only a few of the Six Sigma tools, the contributors will get an appreciation that they are learning the elements of a total methodology. Some of these individuals will then take it on their own to become more familiar with additional Six Sigma tools and begin incorporating these tools into their daily work.

After several years of using Six Sigma and having a team that generated an additional several millions of dollars of savings, I realized that I should revisit the training method and material. This triggered the eventual writing of *Statistics for Six Sigma Made Easy*, which was followed by *All About Six Sigma*. My hope is that this latest book will fill the current void of a practical book on the learning and use of Six Sigma.

PART SEVEN

Miscellaneous Other Six Sigma Tools—Overview

Hodie mihi, cras tibi.   (What's to me today, tomorrow to you.)

—Latin saying

The previous tools in this book were those used by most Six Sigma practitioners. There are several additional tools, however, that have been used successfully by green belts. You should be aware of these tools in case an appropriate need arises. In this book these tools will be discussed only at the level of detail needed to understand their potential. Additional information on how to use these tools can be found in *Statistics for Six Sigma Made Easy* or in the other references listed in the Related Reading and Software.

Process control: Simplified Control Charts are an excellent way to communicate variables process data to an operator. These are discussed in Chapter 22.

Design for Six Sigma: Although design for Six Sigma is often taught separately from traditional Six Sigma, several tools used in design for Six Sigma are often used by green belts in process work. Chapters 23 and 24 discuss these two tools, which are *design of experiments* and *RSS tolerances*.

Simplified Control Charts

Control charts are primarily for those involved in manufacturing or process work and are used in the Control step of the DMAIC process.

Control charts have a chaotic history. In the 1960s, when Japan was showing the United States what quality really meant, the United States tried to implement some quick fixes, which included control charts. Few understood control charts, and they were never used enough to realize their full potential. Now with Six Sigma they are getting a second look, and they have had some impressive successes.

In most cases if a supplier can reduce defect excursions (incidences of higher-than-normal quality issues), the customer will be happy with the product. This does not necessarily mean that all products are within specification. It means that the customer has designed his or her process to work with the normal incoming product. So the emphasis should be on reducing defect excursions, which is the reason control charts were designed.

TRADITIONAL CONTROL CHARTS

Traditional control charts have two graphs. The top graph is based on the process average, with statistically based control rules and limits telling the operator when the process is in or out of control. This graph can't have any reference to the product tolerance because it is displaying product averages. By definition, a tolerance is for individual parts and is meaningless when used on averages.

The second graph on a traditional control chart is based on the process variation (or sigma), also with rules and limits.

If either of these graphs show an out-of-control situation, the operator is supposed to work on the process. However, the charts are somewhat confusing to operators. Sometimes the control chart will show an out-of-control situation while quality checks don't show product out of specification. Also, one graph can show the process as in control while the other shows it out of control.

SIMPLIFIED CONTROL CHARTS

A single chart, as used on the Simplified Control Chart, can give the operator process feedback in a format that is understandable and intuitive and that encourages him or her to react before product is out of specification. It is intuitive because it shows the average and the predicted data spread on one bar. This is the way an operator thinks of his or her process.

Assume that the operator is regularly getting variables data on a critical dimension. Without regular variables data that are entered into some kind of computer or network, control charts are not effective. Refer to the Simplified Control Chart in Figure 22–1 as the following is discussed. Note that setting up this graph will require some computer skills.

Each vertical feedback bar to the operator will be based on the data from the previous 11 product readings. The average $\bar{x}$ and sigma s will be calculated on these 11 readings. The displayed vertical bar will have a small horizontal dash representing the average $\bar{x}$, and the vertical bar will be ± 3 sigma in height from the horizontal average dash.

If the end of a vertical bar crosses a control limit, the vertical bar will be yellow (shown as medium thickness in Figure 22–1). The control limit is midway between the specification and the historical 3 sigma measurements based on a time period when the process was running well. A yellow (shown as medium thickness) bar is the trigger for the operator to review and/or adjust the process.

FIGURE 22–1

Simplified Control Chart

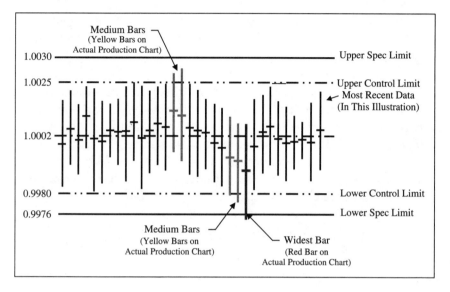

If the vertical bar crosses a specification limit, the vertical bar will be red (shown as widest bar in figure). This communicates to the operator that some of the products are predicted to be out of specification.

A tolerance limit *can* be shown on this chart because the individual part's projected ±3 sigma measurement spread is represented by each vertical line. This is equivalent to having individual data points displayed. However, a control limit is also displayed on this chart, to which the operator has to learn to respond.

Every time a Simplified Control Chart is implemented, there will be many who protest that specific process instructions must be given to the operator on how to bring the process back into control once it goes out. Emphatically no! The operators know how. It may take them some time, but they will do it. They already react when the parts get out of specifications; you just want them to respond somewhat sooner. This quicker reaction often saves them work because it will require only "tweaks" rather than major process changes.

TIP

Use Simplified Control Charts on equipment or process output.

Any piece of equipment or process that makes product that is generally acceptable to the customer, with the exception of defect excursions, is a natural for Simplified Control Charts.

An operator using this kind of control chart will quickly learn that he or she can see trends in either the average or variation and can use that information to help in the debugging process. The information is intuitive and requires little training. This feature is especially critical where personnel changes are frequent. This is a key advantage of the Simplified Control Chart versus the traditional control chart, which is far less intuitive.

Although the most common benefit derived from the Simplified Control Chart is reduced defect excursions, its inherent feedback feature often helps drive process insights and breakthroughs.

CHAPTER 23

Design of Experiments (DOEs)

In an optimized process, all the inputs are at settings that give the best and most stable output. To determine these optimum settings, all key process input variables (KPIVs) must be run at various levels with the results then analyzed to identify which settings give the best results. The methodology to perform this optimization is called a *Simplified Design of Experiments* (DOEs).

This chapter applies to the Improve step in the DMAIC process, and it is primarily for those involved in manufacturing or process work.

Some Six Sigma practitioners feel that DOEs are too complex for someone with green-belt training. These concerns may be valid for traditional DOEs, but the Simplified DOE presented here has been used many times by green belts, with successful results.

First, some discussion on what a DOE entails: It is a controlled test of KPIVs, usually conducted right in the production environment using the actual production equipment. It attempts to measure all possible combinations of KPIVs, rather than taking a standard setup and modifying one variable at a time, one after the other. In this way the DOE attempts to find any interaction among variables and includes this interaction in identifying the optimum settings.

Here are some of the challenges:

1. It is difficult to identify a limited list of KPIVs to test.
2. It is difficult to keep in control the variables *not* being tested. These could include temperature, humidity, and operator skill as well as other variables.

TIP

The results of any DOE are usually *not* the key that drives the process improvement. Instead, it is the disciplined process of setting up and running the test that gives process insight. Observations made during the DOE often trigger process breakthroughs. *Serendipity* becomes dominant in this kind of test.

3. A large number of test variables require many trial iterations and setups.
4. The results of the DOE must then be tested under controlled conditions because the real test of a process change is its ability to predict future results.
5. What to use as an output goal is not a trivial concern. Most software programs limit optimization to one output measurement.

These are the reasons a DOE may scare you; a *Simplified* DOE will minimize these difficulties.

SIMPLIFIED DOE STEPS

Here are the steps to run an effective Simplified DOE:

1. Hold a meeting with a representative from every group familiar with the process. Have the group develop the list of KPIVs and prioritize them.
2. Test combinations of variables. To test two variables A and B, each at two values 1 and 2, there are four possible combinations:

$$A1/B1, \quad A2/B1, \quad A1/B2, \quad A2/B2.$$

To test three variables, each at two values, there are eight combinations:

$$A1/B1/C1, \quad A2/B1/C1, \quad A1/B2/C1, \quad A1/B1/C2,$$
$$A2/B2/C1, \quad A2/B1/C2, \quad A1/B2/C2, \quad A2/B2/C2$$

Each of the above combinations should be run a *minimum* of five times to get a valid statistical average at each iteration. This means that a test of two variables should have a minimum of 4 × 5 = 20 setups and a test of three variables should have a minimum of 8 × 5 = 40 setups.

3. Do each setup independently of the earlier one. Also, make sure that each setup is in random order to reduce any influences of setup order.

Below are the typical results you may see from running a DOE on two variables each at two different settings. We have calculated the average and sigma for each combination:

Group	A1/B1, Inches	A2/B1, Inches	A1/B2, Inches	A2/B2, Inches
Delta average from nominal	0.00023	0.00009	0.00037	0.00020
Sigma on readings	0.00093	0.00028	0.00092	0.00033

The results show that $A2/B1$ had the closest average to the nominal diameter, being off only 0.00009 inch. This group also had the lowest sigma at 0.00028 inch. We would use our earlier statistics to test if this group is statistically different than the next nearest group. If it is, then this would normally be our choice for a controlled run to verify that the results can be duplicated.

If one group had the closest average but a different group had a lower sigma, we would normally go with the lower sigma because the process center (average) can often be easily adjusted.

CHAPTER 24

RSS Tolerance Stack-Ups

Stacked parts are akin to having multiple blocks with each of them placed one block on top of another. When multiple parts were stacked and they had cumulative tolerance buildup, the traditional way to handle the stack-up variation was to assume the worst case on each component—that is, allow for all parts being at the high end of the tolerance or all parts being at the low end of the tolerance.

EXAMPLE OF TRADITIONAL METHOD FOR HANDLING STACK-UP

Assume there is a stack of 9 blocks, each being a nominal 1.000 inch thick, and the tolerance on each part is ±0.003 inch. A traditional worst-case design using this stack of parts would assume the following:

Maximum stack height = 1.003 inches * 9 = 9.027 inches
Minimum stack height = 0.997 inch * 9 = 8.973 inches

The problem with this analysis is that the odds of *all* the parts being at the maximum or *all* the parts being at the minimum are extremely low.

F I G U R E 24–1

Stack of Nine Blocks
Worst-Case and RSS Tolerances

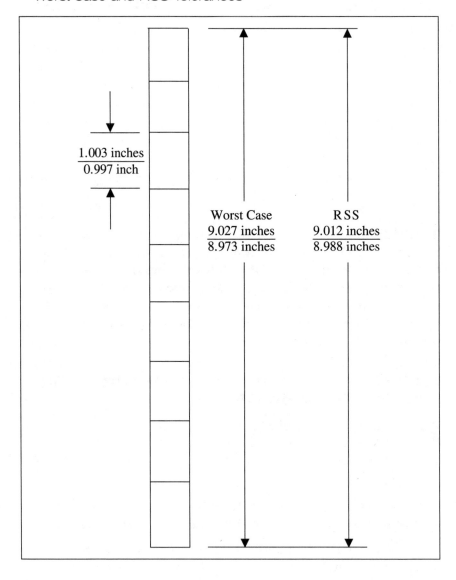

ROOT SUM-OF-SQUARES (RSS) APPROACH TO CALCULATING TOLERANCES

Using the RSS approach on our example, let's calculate what the tolerance should be on the stack of blocks if we assume that ±3 sigma (99.73 percent) of the products are within tolerance:

$$6s = 0.006 \text{ inch (the tolerance)}$$
$$s = 0.001 \text{ inch}$$

The formula to solve for the sigma S of the total stack is the following:

$$S = \sqrt{n(1.3s)^2}$$

In this case, $n = 9$ (number of blocks), $s = 0.001$ inch

So, $S = 0.0039$ inch

So assuming the stack specification is set at ±3 sigma:

Maximum stack height = 9 inches + $3S$ = 9.012 inches
Minimum stack height = 9 inches − $3S$ = 8.988 inches

The comparison between the worst-case assumption and the RSS approach is illustrated in Figure 24–1.

As you can see in the figure, the RSS method resulted in a far tighter tolerance for the stack of parts. This difference could be used in many ways. A looser tolerance could be applied to each block. Or, if the stack were to be used as part of another assembly, the fact of a tighter stack could be used to loosen tolerances in mating parts within that assembly.

The example showed blocks of equal thicknesses, but the same concept can be used on parts of varying thicknesses.

The Six Sigma Statistical Tool Finder Matrix

Look in the need and detail columns in the matrix below to identify the appropriate Six Sigma tool for your project.

Need	Detail	Six Sigma Tool	Location
Address customer needs by identifying and prioritizing actions.	Convert qualitative customer input to specific prioritized actions.	Simplified QFDs	Chapter 6
Minimize collateral damage due to a product or process change.	Convert qualitative input on concerns to specific prioritized actions.	Simplified FMEAs	Chapter 7
Identify key process input variables (KPIVs).	Use expert input on a process.	Cause-and-effect fishbone diagrams	Chapter 8
	Use historical data.	Correlation tests	Chapter 10
Pinpoint possible problem areas of a process.	Use expert input.	Process flow diagrams	Chapter 9
Verify measurement accuracy.	Determine if a gauge is adequate for the task.	Simplified gauge verifications	Chapter 14
Calculate minimum sample size.	Variables (decimal) data.	Sample size, variables	Chapter 17
	Proportional data.	Sample size, proportional	Chapter 18
Determine if there has been a statistically significant change on variables (decimal) data.	Compare a sample to population data.	1. Plot data 2. Chi-square tests 3. *t* tests	Chapter 16 Chapter 17 Chapter 17
	Compare two samples to each other.	1. Plot data 2. *F* tests 3. *t* tests	Chapter 16 Chapter 17 Chapter 17

Need	Detail	Six Sigma Tool	Location
Determine if there has been a statistically significant change on proportional data.	The mathematical probability of the population is known.	*Excel*'s BINOMDIST	Chapter 15
	Compare a sample to a population where both proportions are calculated.	Sample/ population formula	Chapter 18
	Compare two samples where both proportions are calculated.	Sample/sample formula	Chapter 18
Determine if tolerances are appropriate.	How were tolerances determined?	Need-based tolerances	Chapter 11

accuracy   A measurement concept involving the correctness of the average reading. It is the extent to which the average of the measurements taken agrees with a true value.

analyze   The third step in the DMAIC problem-solving method. The measurements and data must be analyzed to see if they are consistent with the problem definition and also to see if they identify a root cause. A problem solution is then identified. Sometimes, based on the analysis, it is necessary to go back and restate the problem definition and start the process over.

attribute   A qualitative characteristic that can be counted. Examples are good or bad, go or no go, and yes or no.

black belt   A person who has earned a Six Sigma black belt and has Six Sigma skills sufficient to act as an instructor, mentor, and expert to green belts. A black belt is also competent in additional Six Sigma tool-specific software programs and statistics.

chi-square test   A test used on variables (decimal) data to see if there is a statistically significant change in the sigma between the population data and the current sample data. This test is conducted only after the data plots have indicated that there has been no radical change in the shape of the data plots.

confidence tests between groups of data   Tests used to determine if there is a statistically significant change between samples or between a sample and a population. These tests are normally done at a 95 percent confidence level.

continuous data   *See* variables data.

control   The final step in the DMAIC problem-solving method. A verification of control must be implemented. A robust solution (like a part change) will be easier to keep in control than a qualitative solution.

correlation testing   A tool that uses historical data to find what variables changed at the same time or position as the problem time or position. These variables are then subjected to further tests or study.

cumulative   In probability problems, the sum of the probabilities of getting "the number of successes or less," like getting 3 *or less* heads on 5 flips of a coin. This option is used on "Less-than" and "More-than" problems.

define   The overall problem definition step in the DMAIC process. The definition should be as specific as possible.

DMAIC problem-solving method: Define, Measure, Analyze, Improve, and Control   The Six Sigma problem-solving approach used by green belts. This is the roadmap that is followed for all projects and process improvements, with the Six Sigma tools applied as needed.

Excel **BINOMDIST**   Not technically a Six Sigma tool but the tool recommended in this book for determining the probability that observed proportional data are the result of purely random causes. This tool is used when we already know the mathematical probability of a population event.

F **test**   A test used on variables (decimal) data to see if there was a statistically significant change in the sigma between two samples. This test is done only after the data plots have indicated that there has been no radical change in the shape of the data plots.

fishbone diagram   A Six Sigma tool that uses a representation of a fish skeleton to help trigger identification of all the variables that can be contributing to a problem. The problem is shown as the fish *head*. The variables are shown on the *bones*. Once all the variables are identified, the key two or three are highlighted for further study.

green belt   A person who has earned a green belt Six Sigma designation and who is the primary implementer or team leader of the Six Sigma methodology. He or she earns this title by taking classes in Six Sigma, demonstrating competency on Six Sigma tests, and implementing Six Sigma projects using the Six Sigma tools.

Improve   The fourth step in the DMAIC problem-solving method. Once a solution has been analyzed, the fix must be implemented. The expected results must be verified with independent data after solution implementation.

labeling averages and standard deviations   The label of the average of a population: $\overline{X}$. The label of the sample average: $\overline{x}$. Similarly, the standard deviation (sigma) of the population is labeled S, and the sample standard deviation (sigma) is labeled s.

master black belt   A person who has earned a Six Sigma master black belt and who generally has management responsibility for the Six Sigma organization. These responsibilities could include setting up training, measuring its effectiveness, coordinating efforts with the rest of the organization, and managing the Six Sigma people (when Six Sigma is set up as a separate organization).

measure   The second step of the DMAIC problem-solving method. Note that accurate and sufficient measurements and data are needed in this step.

minimum sample size   The number of data points needed to enable statistically valid comparisons or predictions.

n   The sample size or, in probability problems, the number of independent trials, like the number of coin tosses or the number of parts measured.

need-based tolerance   A Six Sigma tool that emphasizes that often tolerances are not established based on the customer's real needs. A tolerance review offers opportunity for both the customer and the supplier to save money.

normal distribution   A bell-shaped distribution of data that is indicative of the distribution of data from many things in nature. Information on this type of distribution is used to predict populations based on samples of data.

number *s* (or *x* successes)   The total number of successes that you are looking for in a probability problem, like getting exactly 3 heads. This is used in the *Excel* BINOMDIST program.

plot data   Data plotted on a graph. Most processes with variables data have data plot shapes that stay consistent unless a major change to the process has occurred. If the shapes of the data plots *have* changed dramatically, then the quantitative formulas can't be used to compare the processes.

probability   The likelihood of an event's happening by pure chance.

probability *p* (or probability *s*)   The probability of a success on *each individual trial*, such as the likelihood of a head on one coin flip or a defect on one part. This is always a proportion and generally stated as a decimal, like 0.0156.

probability *P*   In *Excel*'s BINOMDIST, the probability of getting a given number of successes from *all the trials*, like a certain number of heads in a number of coin tosses or a given number of defects in a shipment of parts. This is often the answer in a probability problem.

process flow diagram   A type of flowchart that gives the specific locations or times of process events. A process flow diagram may help pinpoint possible areas contributing to a problem.

proportional data   Data based on attribute inputs, such as good or bad, or stepped numerical data. Examples are the proportion of defects in a process, the proportion of yes votes for a candidate, and the proportion of students failing a test.

repeatability   The consistency of measurements obtained when one person measures a part multiple times with the same device.

reproducibility   The consistency of measurements obtained when two or more people measure a part multiple times with the same device.

sample size, proportional data   A tool used for calculating the minimum sample size needed to get representative attribute data on a process generating proportional data. Too small of a sample may cause erroneous conclusions. Excessively large samples are expensive.

sample size, variables data   A tool used for calculating the minimum sample size needed to get representative data on a process with variables (decimal) data. Too small of a sample may cause erroneous conclusions. Excessively large samples are expensive.

simplified DOE A Six Sigma tool that enables tests to be made on an existing process to establish optimum settings on the key process input variables (KPIVs).

simplified FMEA A Six Sigma tool used to convert qualitative concerns on collateral damage to a prioritized action plan. A planned process or product change may cause unintentional collateral harm to other processes.

simplified gauge verification A Six Sigma tool used on variables data (decimals) to verify that the gauge is capable of giving the required accuracy of measurements compared to the allowable tolerance.

simplified QFD A Six Sigma tool used to convert qualitative customer input into specific prioritized action plans. The "customer" is anyone who is affected by the product or process.

Six Sigma methodology A *specific problem-solving approach* that uses *Six Sigma tools* to improve processes and products. This methodology is data driven, and the goal is to reduce unacceptable products or events. The technical Six Sigma goal is to reduce defects to no more than 3 defects per million parts. The real-world Six Sigma goal is to reduce defects to the level at which the customer is happy with the product, supplier losses are low, and economics can't justify further improvement.

t **test** A Six Sigma test used to see if there is a statistically significant change in the average between population data and the current sample data, or between two samples. This test on variables data is done only after the data plots have indicated that there has been no radical change in the shapes of the data plots and the chi-square test or *F* test shows no significant change in sigma.

variables data Continuous data that are generally in decimal form. Theoretically you could look at enough decimal places to find that no two values are exactly the same.

RELATED READING

Berk, Kenneth N., and Patrick Carey. *Data Analysis with Microsoft Excel.* (Southbank, Australia, and Belmont, Calif.: Brooks/Cole, 2004.)

Brussee, Warren T. *Statistics for Six Sigma Made Easy.* (New York: McGraw-Hill, 2004.)

Capinski, Marek, and Tomasz Zastawniak. *Probability Through Problems.* (New York: Springer-Verlag, 2001.)

Cohen, Louis. *Quality Function Deployment: How to Make QFD Work for You.* (Upper Saddle River, N.J.: Prentice-Hall PTR, 1995.)

Harry, Mikel J., and Richard Schroeder. *Six Sigma: The Breakthrough Management Strategy Revolutionizing the World's Top Corporations.* (New York: Random House/Doubleday/Currency, 1999.)

Harry, Mikel J., and Reigle Stewart. *Six Sigma Mechanical Design Tolerancing,* 2nd ed. (Scaumburg, Ill.: Motorola University Press, 1988.)

Hoerl, Roger W., and Ronald D. Snee. *Statistical Thinking: Improving Business Performance.* (Pacific Grove, Calif.: Duxbury-Thomson Learning, 2002.)

Jaisingh, Lloyd R. *Statistics for the Utterly Confused.* (New York: McGraw-Hill, 2000.)

Kiemele, Mark J., Stephen R. Schmidt, and Ronald J. Berdine. *Basic Statistics, Tools for Continuous Improvement,* 4th ed. (Colorado Springs, Colo.: Air Academy Press, 1997.)

Levine, David M., and David Stephan, Timothy C. Krehbiel, and Mark L. Berenson. *Statistics for Managers, Using Microsoft Excel (with CD-ROM),* 4th ed. (Upper Saddle River, N.J.: Prentice-Hall, 2004.)

McDermott, Robin E., Raymond J. Mikulak, and Michael R. Beauregard. *The Basics of FMEA.* (New York: Quality Resources, 1996.)

Mizuno, Shigeru, and Yoji Akao, editors. *QFD: The Customer-Driven Approach to Quality Planning and Deployment.* (Tokyo: Asian Productivity Organization, 1994.)

Montgomery, Douglas C. *Design and Analysis of Experiments,* 5th ed. (New York: Wiley, 2001.)

Pande, Peter S., Robert P. Neuman, and Roland R. Cavanagh. *The Six Sigma Way: How GE, Motorola, and Other Top Companies Are Honing Their Performance.* (New York: McGraw-Hill, 2000.)

Pyzdek, Thomas. *The Six Sigma Handbook, Revised and Expanded: The Complete Guide for Greenbelts, Blackbelts, and Managers at All Levels.* (New York: McGraw-Hill, 2003.)

Rath & Strong Management Consultants. *Rath & Strong's Six Sigma Pocket Guide.* (New York: McGraw-Hill, 2003.)

Schmidt, Stephen R., and Robert G. Launsby. *Understanding Industrial Designed Experiments (with CD-ROM)*, 4th ed. (Colorado Springs, Colo.: Air Academy Press, 1997.)

Smith, Dick, and Jerry Blakeslee. *Strategic Six Sigma: Best Practices from the Executive Suite*. (Hoboken, N.J.: Wiley, 2002.)

Stamatis, D. H. *Failure Mode & Effect Analysis: FMEA from Theory to Execution*, 2nd ed. (Milwaukee: American Society for Quality, 2003.)

Swinscow, T. D. V., and M. J. Cambell. *Statistics at Square One*, 10th ed. (London: BMJ Books, 2001.)

SOFTWARE

Crystal Ball 2000. (Denver, Colo.: Decisioneering, Inc., www.decisioneering.com).

Minitab 14. (State College, Penn.: Minitab Inc., www.Minitab.com).

Relex FMES/FMECA. (Greensburg, Penn.: Relex Software Corporation, www.relexsoftware.com).

Warren Brussee spent 33 years at GE as an engineer, plant manager, and engineering manager. His responsibilities included manufacturing plants in the United States, Hungary, and China.

Mr. Brussee is a Six Sigma green belt, and he has taught Six Sigma classes to engineering and manufacturing teams. These teams excelled both on company-administered tests of Six Sigma and in actual implementation of the Six Sigma tools. Mr. Brussee has also done Six Sigma consulting with various companies.

Mr. Brussee has multiple patents, and some were the outcome of his Six Sigma work. His teams generated several million dollars' worth of annualized savings using the Six Sigma tools.

Mr. Brussee earned his engineering degree at Cleveland State University and attended Kent State University toward an EMBA.

Mr. Brussee wrote his earlier book, *Statistics for SIX SIGMA Made Easy*, to make the statistics involved with Six Sigma user-friendly and to introduce the Six Sigma methodology with a set of simplified tools. *All About Six Sigma* uses the same philosophy to make the whole methodology of Six Sigma easier to implement and understand.